HOW TO LIVE DANGEROUSLY

Warwick Cairns was born in Dagenham in 1962.
He studied English at Yale under Harold Bloom,
has travelled in the deserts of northern Kenya with
Wilfred Thesiger and worked drilling wells on a
Sioux reservation in South Dakota. He lives in
Windsor with his wife and two daughters.
This is his second book.

Also by Warwick Cairns

About the Size of It

WARWICK CAIRNS

HOW TO LIVE DANGEROUSLY

WHY WE SHOULD ALL STOP WORRYING, AND START LIVING

MACMILLAN

First published 2008 by Macmillan
an imprint of Pan Macmillan Ltd
Pan Macmillan, 20 New Wharf Road, London N1 9RR
Basingstoke and Oxford
Associated companies throughout the world
www.panmacmillan.com

ISBN 978-0-230-71221-8

1 3 5 7 9 8 6 4 2

A CIP catalogue record for this book is available from
the British Library.

Printed and bound in the Uk by
CPI Mackays, Chatham ME5 8TD

Visit **www.panmacmillan.com** to read more about all our books
and to buy them. You will also find features, author interviews and
news of any author events, and you can sign up for e-newsletters
so that you're always first to hear about our new releases.

For Sue, Alice and Lucy

CONTENTS

INTRODUCTION

This is a book about the dangers of life, and how we face up to them. Or rather, it's a book about how we fail to face up to them these days.

In this book you will find out why we worry too much about some things, and why we don't worry enough about others. You will learn more about how we've stopped letting our children go out to play, and why, as a consequence, they are growing up fat, unhealthy and unhappy. And you will see more clearly the many ways in which we give up responsibility for our own actions and allow ourselves to be ordered about by ever more ludicrous and intrusive new laws and regulations – laws and regulations which are passed, in the most part, by bossy and self-important individuals who think that they know better than we do how we should be allowed to live our lives.

It's something of a journey, this book, and it sets off from some of the more unusual fears and obsessions of our age and goes all the way to the structure and function of the human brain and beyond, by way of frivolous law-suits, the chemicals in burnt toast, some confessions of childhood foolishness, the family tree of Genghis Khan, the traffic system of the Dutch town of Drachten, a rather unwise experiment you can do with an arrow and some tips to help you do better at any dangerous sports you may happen to take part in.

The gist of it all, though, is that we all ought to stop worrying so much about things, and that we ought to get out and live a bit more, and take a few more risks. And it follows from this that if you take the advice given in this book, bad things will happen to you. That's what happens, you see, when you take risks.

But you should also find, if you follow the advice in this book, that many, many more good things will happen to you by way of recompense; and they will be things that will make you feel intensely and passionately alive, right here and right now.

PART ONE

RUN, HIDE, SAVE YOURSELVES!

A SHORT INTRODUCTION TO MODERN FEARS

There are any number of places to start a journey into danger. But we will start ours in the brightly lit dressing-room of a provincial theatre somewhere on the east coast of England.

Imagine this, ladies and gentlemen, boys and girls: imagine. Imagine that you, personally, are Widow Twanky, the famous pantomime dame.

If you take a look, right now, in your mirror, you will see that your face has been powdered and painted into the most grotesque caricature of a lady of mature years. You will have big arched eyebrows stretching halfway up your forehead, oversized cupid's-bow lips, round red apple-cheeks and a beauty spot; on your head you will have a hot, itchy woollen wig with great plaited coils over your ears. And then, of course, there will be your clothes – an appalling dog's dinner of a milkmaid's dress, all clashing spots and checks and tartans and gingham patches; and finally, looped over your arm . . . well, looped over your arm you will be carrying what is known in the gardening world as a 'trug', which is a sort of shallow basket with a hooped handle, and in this trug you will see sweets – heaps and heaps of sugar and chocolate confectionery.

Armed with your trug, you make your way on stage, singing loudly and out of tune in your best falsetto screech, and then you say some lines and have a bit of banter with the audience, going through some business about where something or other is – a young woman dressed up in a furry suit, say, pretending to be a cat – and you cup your hand to your ear as the audience all yell IT'S BEHIND YOU! but you always manage to turn round just that split second too late to see it. And then, after a while, comes the sweet-throwing moment. The children have all been waiting for this, and you can see the expectation in their eyes. You reach down and grab a handful of the things and swing your arm back, ready to hurl them into the audience, when all of a sudden who should appear on stage but an angry-looking little man in a suit, carrying a clipboard.

'You can't do that,' he says. 'You can't throw those sweets to the boys and girls.'

'Oh yes I can,' you say.

'Oh no you can't,' he says.

'OH YES I CAN,' you say.

'Stop that,' he says. 'And you, too,' he adds, turning to the audience.

He stoops to inspect the contents of your basket.

'You could have someone's eye out with one of those,' he says, picking up a mint humbug.

'OH NO I COULDN'T,' you say, but he's having none of it. This is a serious matter, he says. Because although, as it turns out, there has never been a recorded case of anyone having their eye taken out or being otherwise seriously injured by the throwing of sweets in pantomimes in all the years in all the centuries since pantomimes and sweets were first invented, this doesn't make it safe. Oh no: it *could* happen, you see, the eye-taking-out thing – there's always a first time for everything. For this reason, the management has instituted a new policy for the distribution of sweets: as Widow Twanky, you are now required to drop them carefully into a box on the floor in the front row, from where usherettes will collect them and distribute them safely and sensibly to the waiting children.

In 2007, at the Gorleston Pavilion Theatre in Norfolk, sweet-throwing was banned after insurers warned the management that they could be sued if anyone was hurt by flying confectionery.[1] In the same year, at the Gaiety Theatre in Ayr, a similar ban was put in place after a pack of wine-gums hit a light. A council spokesman said: 'The health and safety of audiences is paramount, so a decision has been taken that sweets will no longer be thrown into the audience.'

Across the country, other theatres followed suit. In theatre after theatre sweet-throwing was either banned altogether or else – as in the Forum Theatre in Billingham – allowed subject only to a carefully controlled risk-limitation policy by which sweets could still be thrown, but only underarm and only if they were very soft and light, and not capable of having anyone's eye out. Marshmallows, say, or those rice-paper flying-saucer things with the sherbet in the middle. But not hard, dangerous projectiles like lemon bonbons or mint humbugs. And definitely not gobstoppers – especially the extra-large ones. Now those *would* hurt, wouldn't they? And reading this, you might say to yourself, 'Well, if I were running a theatre, I'd make damn sure that my Widow Twanky could throw all the sweets she liked – in fact, I'd order her to throw more!' But would you? If you had officials and insurance-assessors breathing down your neck, threatening you with goodness-knows-what financial consequences, would you really say 'Stuff you! We're throwing sweets and that's that!'?

We live in worried times. For all sorts of reasons, both

good and bad, more people today are more worried about the dangers of life than at any time in history. Previous generations might have had to cope with continual war, grinding poverty, the constant presence of pestilence and famine, and even then – even if they survived their own birth, which was by no means certain, and even if they managed to avoid the ravages of scurvy and the Black Death – they still lived little longer than the average domestic flea. But it is today that people are *really* worried.

This is a fact, confirmed again and again by research all over the world. Survey after survey has shown that most people nowadays believe the world to be a far more dangerous place than it was in the past, and they're not happy about it. Depending on the survey, and depending on the country, between 75 and 80 per cent think this is true. (In the USA, one source puts the figure at 78 per cent;[2] in Britain, an ICM poll suggests 79 per cent.[3])

Today there seem to be all sorts of new threats arising, and all sorts of bad people and bad things out to get us and our children. To name a few at random: terrorism; violent crime; newer, more addictive drugs; binge-drinking; passive smoking; global warming and its associated floods, famine and extinction; 'stranger danger'; traffic fumes; the side effects of food additives and vaccinations; the rise in allergies and 'intolerances'; antibiotic-resistant 'superbugs' in hospitals; AIDS; bird flu; skin-cancer from being in the sun; 'obesity epidemics' from staying indoors; cancer from mobile phone-mast radiation; bullying in schools; teenage boys with guns and knives; teenage girls with eating disorders; third-world dictators with nuclear weapons . . .

Because of all this, and more, many people have stopped doing, or changed the way they do, many of the things they did when they were younger, because they are now considered too dangerous. 'You just can't do that any more,' they say. 'Not like you used to when we were young.'

Go to the theatre and you worry about the dangers of sweet-throwing; let your children play out in the street and you worry about all the abductors or worse hiding round the corner, waiting to snatch them away, or the maniac drivers revving up their engines, waiting to run them over, or the hooded gangs of feral teenagers, waiting to rob them or beat them up, or both; go out for a bite to eat and there's a whole range of things to worry about, from gluten and lactose intolerances to cholesterol and pesticide residues.

Every year, the private health-care company BUPA publishes a research document it calls the 'Worry Report'[4], which tracks the fears and concerns of the British public.

What this report shows is a growing trend of anxiety. Not only do most people think that the world has become a more dangerous place, but well over half of all adults now say that they actively worry much more than they did even five years ago. A fifth of all British adults, meanwhile, worry so much, and so often, that they regularly lose sleep and/or their appetite as a result.

While terrorism and climate change are major concerns for many, what people worry particularly about are threats to health, both their own and that of their family. Anxiety has reached such a level that more and more of us are tipping over the edge and developing full-blown pathological fears or phobias.

According to a report published by Britain's National Phobics Society in 2007,[5] the number of people suffering from phobias is rising sharply, and it has now reached the point where one person in eight suffers from at least one phobia. And some people have many, many more. It's telling, too, that in an age of health scares, the kind of phobias that people suffer from is changing. It used to be that the most common ones were the 'old favourites', the ones with the Greek names such as claustrophobia (fear of enclosed spaces) or agoraphobia (fear of open spaces) or arachnophobia (the fear of spiders). Now these old phobias have been overtaken by a whole new set of fears, many of which don't even have names yet – or at least, they don't have names that most people have heard of. They tend to be health related and often to do with dirt and germs. For example, according to the report, at least 4 million people in the UK alone suffer from a powerful fear of germs in lavatories, particularly public or shared ones. Which probably goes some way towards explaining why so many new houses have so many bathrooms in them. That and the fact that it seems to have become the norm for people to take a bath or a shower every single day, and in some cases even more often, rather than, say, whenever they get particularly dirty. I wonder what they do when they really have to go, these people with the toilet phobia? Hold it in as long as they can, I suppose, and then scrub their hands with antibacterial soap afterwards.

Lavatories aside, people also get very worried about the germs they might pick up by touching things in shops and other public places. Because of this, there is a growing market for products such as the Healthy Handle which is, according to its makers, 'doctor-recommended for use on filthy, germ-infested shopping-cart handles'. It's a sort of extendable plastic sheath that clips over the handle of a supermarket trolley to avoid the terrors of having to touch the handle itself. When you've finished with it, you simply unclip it and pop it in your bag – along with the germs you were trying to avoid by using it, presumably. This seems something of a design flaw to me, but what do I know? Alternatively, or additionally, you can carry a pack of Nice 'n' Clean antibacterial surface wipes, which are specifically recommended for shopping-trolley handles. And if you have babies or small children who might want to ride in the trolley along with the shopping, you can always buy the CartSafari shopping-trolley cover with Microban, which covers the seat, handle and side-bars of the trolley with antibacterial fabric to prevent your child touching anything at all unclean.

These things didn't exist a generation ago, when people were less fussy about dirt. If they had, their market would have been limited to a few eccentric recluses like the germophobic millionaire Howard Hughes; now, they're increasingly sold as mainstream products for everyday people.

All of which leads us to another question: if we're all so anxious these days about the possibility that bad things might happen to us, how do we cope when those bad things actually come to pass?

WHY IT'S NEVER YOUR OWN STUPID FAULT

At an advertising agency where I used to work, one of the more high-powered account executives slipped, one day, on the stairs coming down from a fifth-floor meeting room and came down several steps rather more quickly than she had anticipated, on her backside.

This came as a bit of a surprise to her.

She slipped on those stairs not because she was clumsy, or because she was wearing expensive high-heeled shoes, and certainly not because she was trying to find her wafer-thin mobile phone in her oversized patent-leather handbag while not paying enough attention to where she was going, but because of the stairs themselves, which made her fall, on account of being unduly shiny or slippery or something.

She was quite sure of that fact, and if it was also a fact that lots of other people had managed to get down those same stairs that day in the normal way, without any trouble, then that was neither here nor there: the fact was that she had fallen. Moreover, in falling she had suffered Soft Tissue Damage.

Soft Tissue Damage might sound like a fancy phrase for a painful and embarrassing bruise, but it is not the same thing at all. Painful and embarrassing bruises go away by themselves, but Soft Tissue Damage only goes away after a course of expensive private physiotherapy, the bill for which was duly presented to the Managing Director some days later.

It's worth knowing this.

I wish I'd known it myself a couple of months before when, at the age of forty-five, I thought it would be a good idea to learn to ride a BMX bike.

There are a lot of things you can do on a BMX bike at my age, or indeed at any age, besides looking really stupid. One of them is what's known as a manual. A manual is a kind of wheelie, where you go up on your back wheel, but it's called a manual and not a wheelie because instead of pedalling, as in a normal wheelie, you pull the front of the bike up manually while leaning back and down over the back wheel. So anyway, you do this pulling and leaning until you reach a crucial balance point, riding along on your back wheel, and you shift your weight and touch your back brake to keep yourself in balance. Or at least, that is the theory of it.

What I discovered, while trying to learn this manual thing one lunchtime in central London, is an addition to the theory: what happens if you keep on pulling and leaning back beyond the balance point, at speed, and beyond the point at which you can get your feet down on the ground and run out of it.

What happens is that you topple over backwards. If you topple over backwards on a bike with your hands still on the handlebars and your feet still on the pedals, you land with all of your weight on your backside, watched by appreciative passers-by, and then your bike shoots off without you and smacks into the side of a parked car, denting it on impact and then taking a big gouge out of the paintwork as it skids away. I also discovered that when you try to get up after something like this, it sometimes happens that one of your legs decides it doesn't want to comply, and you find yourself mouthing the same swear-word over and over again to yourself out of pain and humiliation as you struggle to your feet and limp over to pick up your bike. You will experience difficulty in walking for some days afterwards, I found, and your leg will seize up if you sit still for any length of time, so that to get up again you have to brace your arms against a table or something solid and pull yourself to your feet. After a few days of this, there will appear what you might take, at first glance, to be the most monstrous black bruise you have ever seen. That, at any rate, was what I took it for; but if I had known then what I know now, I would have known that it was actually Soft Tissue Damage, and Soft Tissue Damage is something for which someone else is always to blame, and for which someone else ought to have paid compensation.

And this, it seems, is another of the great emerging themes of modern life. If it is true that we worry more and more about bad things happening to us, it is also true that when bad things do happen, we try to avoid responsibility for them wherever possible. We blame others for getting us into the mess we are in, and we expect others to get us out of it, and make everything all right.

Let me give you some other examples of what I mean.

Imagine that you have booked an exotic holiday, to the Dominican Republic, and you are lying there on your towel under a coconut tree on the white sand beach (or whatever colour sand they have over there) under the cloudless blue sky, listening to the waves lapping against the shore, or, at least, to the sounds of your fellow holidaymakers, when all of a sudden a bloody great coconut falls out of the tree, as coconuts are wont to do, and lands smack on your chest, or thump-crack on your chest, as the case may be. Whose fault is that, eh?

Is it your fault for lying under a tree heavy with coconuts, or is it someone else's? And, in the circumstances, what do you do? What you do – or at least, what one holiday-maker did, according to a news report in 2000 – is you blame the holiday company: you sue them for damages and you receive a large out-of-court settlement.

Got the hang of that? Another one – an easy one, this time. You are what the Americans call a 'young person of size' and you got that way by stuffing your face with cheese-burgers, quarter-pounders 'n' fries, chicken McNuggets and extra-large, extra-thick chocolate shakes. However, for most of your life neither you nor any member of your family has had any idea that your size has anything whatsoever to do with the amount of junk food you've been pigging. Suddenly, one day, you discover the truth. The scales fall from your eyes. Eating like a glutton has made you put on weight and threatens your health and wellbeing! Not to mention your ability to walk through doorways without turning sideways. Who would have believed it? So what do you do? Yep – you sue McDonald's.[6] Perhaps you sue them for millions of dollars, in the hope of outdoing Stella Liebeck, the woman who was initially awarded $2.9 million by an American jury after she put a cup of hot McDonald's coffee on her lap in the car and then, when it spilt and scalded her, sued and won[7] (though the final, undisclosed amount settled upon is still a matter of dispute).

It's quite a fun game, this. You could turn it into a competitive sport for the Olympics and it would easily hold its own alongside the likes of synchronized swimming and beach volleyball. You could build a stadium for it, at vast public expense, and then knock it down after the week or so it's used for, and then blame someone else for wasting all that money. The aim of this game, competitive suing, is to give as breathtaking a performance as possible, aiming for the highest levels of audacity and shamelessness you can manage, combined with the lowest possible levels of irony and self-awareness.

You are a teenager and you don't do very well in your exams: you sue your school.

You are a convict serving twenty-three years in prison: you sue *yourself* for $5 million for violating your own civil rights and religious beliefs by allowing yourself to get drunk and commit crimes, in the hope that, since you have no income, the state will pay the compensation instead. (This actually happened, in Virginia in 1993. The case was thrown out of court.)

You've got the point now, I think. If I start boring you by labouring it for too long, you can sue me. And I'll sue you back for mental anguish.

I just want to finish this bit with two world-class performances, to show you the sort of thing you should be aiming for.

A young woman from London was celebrating her twenty-fourth birthday, with friends, in her shared flat. Around midnight, when she had consumed 'four or five' glasses of wine and a vodka jelly, she and a group of partygoers decided to climb out of her upstairs window and onto the roof of some adjoining garages, to continue the party there, and no doubt to cheer up her sleeping neighbours with the sounds of jollity, mirth and loud music. By accident, she stood on a flimsy perspex skylight which gave way and sent her plummeting to the ground below, where she sustained some pretty nasty injuries. Whose fault was that, do you think? And who was wholly to blame? And what do you think she did? Correct: she blamed the owners of the garage and sued them for negligence.[8]

Finally, I want to tell you the story of a Sunderland greyhound trainer by the name of Graham Calvert, who discovered that he rather enjoyed gambling. He enjoyed it so much that he went through an astonishing amount of money and then did the honourable thing: he sued the bookmaker, William Hill, for £2,052,972 for letting him do it. It wasn't his fault, you see: the company had failed in its 'duty of care' by allowing him to carry on betting. He lost his case.[9]

That's it for compensation cases, but I want to pick up on this idea about 'disorders' and how they fit into a world where people increasingly offload the responsibility for the consequences of their own actions.

Medical-sounding terminology is always a good bet for doing that. It sounds better and less blameworthy to be 'dyspraxic' than clumsy, better and less blameworthy to 'suffer from depression' than to feel a bit down in the dumps about your life, better and less blameworthy for your child to have 'attention deficit hyperactivity disorder' than to be rude and naughty. It makes you sound like a victim of circumstances beyond your control. You don't have to sort your life out or face up to your problems: you can just get a doctor to give you some pills instead.

You're not a spectacularly feckless idiot if you gamble to excess, you see: you've got a 'disorder'. You're not fat because you eat too much and sit around on your enormous backside: you're fat because you've caught fatness from the 'obesity epidemic'. Which has about as much medical basis to it as the flared-trouser epidemic of the 1970s or the opium-addiction epidemic in China that miraculously cured itself overnight after Mao Tse-tung issued a proclamation to the effect that anyone found in possession of opium would be shot, and executed a few addicts to demonstrate what he meant.[10] Although Dr Hamish Meldrum, the head of the British Medical Association, was swiftly shot down by obesity campaigners for allegedly speaking a few home truths about making 'diseases' out of lifestyle choices. According to Dr Meldrum, 'We are tending to say, "This patient has a hyper-appetite problem" rather than maybe they are eating too much.' And, he added, 'People like to put fancy labels that suggest things are a medical problem.'[11] In fact, he says, they're not. This is not to say that glands and genes don't have a role to play in how much you can eat before you put on weight, and no one denies that some people can eat buckets of cream cakes and stay thin, while others seem to get fat just by looking at food, but that's just the luck of the draw. If you've got 'fat genes' it's a nuisance, but you just have to eat less.

Sorry, that was a bit of a rant, wasn't it? You can disagree with me if you like. But why not have a go yourself? Using your own skill and judgement, decide how much sympathy you ought to have for former soccer star George Best, a man with a millionaire lifestyle, good looks, a prodigious talent, a string of Miss World-style lady companions and the adoration of millions, but who, unfortunately, fell victim to the disease of alcoholism. Or else, who foolishly, and in full knowledge of what he was doing, drank himself to oblivion and ultimately, to death. The choice is yours.

So this is where we've come to, so far: we're getting more anxious about bad things happening to us and we increasingly seek to avoid responsibility when bad things actually happen. We prefer, instead, that others take responsibility for our actions.

Fortunately – or unfortunately – there are people out there, whole committees of people, only too willing to take on that kind of responsibility, and whose mission it is to decide for us how we ought to live our lives, and to tell us which kinds of risks we are allowed to take and which ones we aren't. These people are to be found everywhere, running things. They run schools and they run councils, they run institutions and they run governments.

They are the rule-makers, the experts, the legislators, the authorities. They are the People Who Know What's Good for You.

THE PEOPLE WHO KNOW WHAT'S GOOD FOR YOU

Imagine, for a moment, that you are a vet – a rural vet, in rugged hill-country: Yorkshire, say – and imagine that in your capacity as a vet, you spend a lot of your time visiting remote farms to deal with sheep and cattle and the like, and a good deal of your work involves shoving your arm up to the shoulder in a cow's backside, while old boys in navy overalls with orange baling-twine for belts and tweed flat caps on their heads stand by, passing dry and not altogether favourable comments on how your performance compares with that of the previous incumbent of your practice.

You do this, day in and day out, for month after month and year after year. You get called out at all sorts of unsociable hours. You spend many hours every day negotiating narrow country roads and farm tracks in your car and, after a while, you feel the need for a bit of companionship on your travels. Being the sort of person you are, and having been interested in animals for as long as you can remember, you get yourself a dog – a border collie given you as a pup by a grateful farmer, say – and, like generations of vets before you, you take him with you on your rounds. And after a while you become inseparable. He knows and anticipates your needs and moods, and you his.

Now, these farms you're visiting, you aren't going there for fun, or to brush up on your bovine proctology skills: you're going there, by and large, because the farmer has a problem; and often this problem involves disease of some kind. So, your dog: you probably aren't going to let him go rushing off ahead of you to have a sniff round among the infected animals and a good old roll in their droppings. You're probably going to leave him in your car. And if it's a hot day, you probably aren't going to park your car in direct sunlight with the windows all closed and without leaving your dog anything to drink. You would act with consideration for the potential for cross-infection, and with concern for the comfort and wellbeing of your travelling companion. Being a vet, and having trained for however many years it is, you'd know all that without anyone having to tell you, and you'd know it better and more instinctively than almost anyone else in the world: it would be second nature to you.

In 2007 the British government passed new legislation forbidding vets from taking their dogs with them to visit farms or on any other 'official business', in case they should leave them in their cars in hot weather or in case the dogs should compromise 'bio-security'.[12]

The result of this was that shortly after the legislation took effect, a number of rural vets resigned rather than be parted from their companions, and rather than leave the dogs on their own for hours on end at home, wondering what they had done wrong to be banished from the company of their owner.

Everyone else, meanwhile, is still allowed to take as many dogs as they like from farm to farm, and to let them run where they will, or else keep them cooped up in cars for as long as they like, whatever the weather; just not vets.

As legislation goes, you might consider this piece to be hamfisted, or inflexible, or unduly prescriptive. From the point of view of animal welfare, you may consider it to be self-defeating – at least as far as the welfare of vets' dogs is concerned. But the most important thing about it, whether it's good or bad legislation, is the fact that it's legislation at all. It's legislation moving into areas where no legislation was considered necessary before, and it compels people to do, by law, what once they were free to do – or not do – for themselves, by exercising their own skill and judgement.

There's a lot of this sort of thing going on these days. You might ask why we put up with it, and why we allow our freedom of action to be taken over by the authorities; but to a large extent we are all complicit. To a large extent, handing over responsibility to the people in charge and the people who know best is what many of us want.

If you look, for example, at the way we use the emergency services, you will see that there has been a fundamental change in the past decade or two. At one time, dialling 999 on your telephone – if you had one – was something you did as an absolute last resort, if your house was on fire, say, or if you'd been burgled, or if you'd been run over by a horse-drawn tram – or preferably all three at once. And even then, if you weren't actually likely to die within the next half-hour, you thought twice about calling, in case you were told off for wasting the authorities' time.

These days, an emergency call is often seen as a first port of call for more or less anything you happen to be worried about. Official estimates vary from region to region, but it is accepted that anywhere between a third and four-fifths of all calls to the police, the fire brigade and the ambulance service are completely unnecessary.

Records show teenagers calling for help in finding mis-placed mobile phones; expectant fathers requesting ambulances to take their pregnant wives to hospital while they wait in for a pizza to be delivered; people complaining that their Chinese takeaways are cold; and people requesting urgent medical attention for constipation, or for getting soap in their eyes.

Hospital accident-and-emergency units, meanwhile, are overwhelmed by anxious parents of children with minor ailments which, properly, are much better dealt with at home, with a plaster or a 'make-better kiss' and a comfy bed, followed perhaps by a visit to the GP the next day. Things like a fever, for example, or a nasty bruise. And, according to the head of the Royal College of Paediatrics and Child Health, few of these parents are content for their child to be attended to by a nurse or even a junior doctor. They want, they demand, to see a consultant paediatrician at the very least.[13]

So private problems are increasingly problems for which we turn to the authorities for help.

And increasingly, whenever something unpleasant and unfortunate happens – a child is savaged by a fierce dog, for example, or a madman runs amok with a handgun – there is a clamour from the public and from the media for tough new laws to prevent it ever happening again.

Given that passing laws and making rules and regulations is what the people in charge are paid to do, it is not exactly surprising that they start doing so. So whole breeds of dogs get banned, and all handguns get banned, whoever owns them, and however unlikely they are to harm anyone or anything, ever; and the British Olympic shooting team are no longer allowed to practise in their home country, and have to do it in Switzerland instead.

We are all, these days, measurably more beset by rules and regulations, and by policies and procedures designed to keep us out of harm's way, to protect us from our own and others' follies and to save us from the caprices of fate and nature, than mankind has ever been before.

It's easy to mock some of those rules. In fact, to show you how easy it is, I'm going to do just that. It's easier than easy to come up with examples of 'health-and-safety madness' so outrageously bonkers that you'd find it hard to make up anything sillier yourself. People talk about setting up straw men to knock down, but here you don't even have to do the setting up: some earnest, po-faced public official has already done it for you – following the correct straw-man-building procedures, of course, using approved fire-resistant artificial straw and wearing the appropriate safety equipment.

Step forward Swindon Council, who informed an

author who wanted to sell his books on council premises that he must take out multimillion-pound public liability insurance. According to council spokeswoman Victoria Tagg, 'The high number of claims made against organizations and individuals these days means that no one offering products or services for sale, no matter how minor, can afford to be without public liability insurance.[14]

Step forward security company First Management Group, for sacking an employee for 'a serious breach of health and safety regulations'. The employee in question had climbed some scaffolding to rescue a suicidal patient at Lewisham hospital.

Step forward Bristol City Council for reclassifying doormats as 'tripping hazards' and instructing all of the tenants in its flats to remove them immediately.

And step forward all the many others, far, far too numerous to mention here in their entirety, but who include Chelmsford Cathedral for replacing its choristers' candles with 'glow-sticks' to save them from going up in flames; Crudwell Church of England Primary School for banning home-made cakes from its cake sales to shield buyers from the risk of salmonella; Bournemouth authorities for banning its district nurses from riding bikes on account of it being too dangerous; Worcester Council for reportedly erecting plastic barriers and

'Warning, Pears Falling' signs around fifty-year-old pear trees in Cripplegate Park on account of Pear Danger;[15] and Tesco for banning children's entertainer Barney Baloney from making balloon animals on their premises (potential latex allergies).[16]

You get the point.

I ought to stop now.

I really ought to, but it gets addictive.

You can see why the popular newspapers love this stuff so much.

So, just a couple more, then.

The Conker Safety Goggle Man: have I mentioned him yet? More or less everyone else has, but it's such a good one that I'm not planning to let that fact stop me. Conkers, for the benefit of overseas readers or hermits, is a British children's game. You collect your conkers – the big, shiny seeds of the horse chestnut tree – thread one onto a shoelace and then whack your friend's conker with it, and he or she whacks yours, until one breaks. And that's it. It's not quite three-dimensional chess, but it's fairly harmless. Not harmless enough, though, for the headmaster of Cummersdale Primary School in Cumbria, who decided that any child playing conkers in his school should wear big plastic safety goggles, like scientists wear in laboratories, in case a bit of flying conker had one of their eyes out, for just about the first time in however many hundred years the game's been played.

The Cummersdale man isn't the only big name in conker concern. There's Gary Postlethwaite, headmaster of Bookwell Primary School in Cumberland, who, in response to parent pressure, banned conkers altogether in case they might set off nut allergies. All this worry despite the fact that the Anaphylaxis Campaign say that in all the years they've been going they've never come across a single case of an allergic reaction to conkers.

And then there is Newcastle City Council, who, because of the safety concerns of local residents, employed teams of workers to strip conkers from trees in the city before children could hurt themselves collecting them.[17]

All of these people, no doubt, had their reasons for doing what they did. Throwing heavy sticks up into a tree probably isn't the safest thing in the world, especially from the point of view of passers-by. This has always been so – it was true when I threw sticks into a tree as a child, and true when my father and grandfather did it. But it's only now that this kind of 'preventative action' is becoming the norm.

I could go on, and go on at some length, but that would be pure self-indulgence, so I won't. There are other things, important things, that we need to talk about.

The first of those things is the fact that right here and right now we are living through a time of profound and unprecedented change in the way we deal with the world.

It's not actually about the merits of candles or door-mats, this thing, or about dogs on farms or conkers or any other individual instance: it's about who decides. It's about the way we live; it's about the things we do; and it's about the power we have to take our own chances and make our own choices in life, for good or ill.

To the question, 'Who has the main responsibility for my own safety and wellbeing?' the answer used to be, 'I do'. Now it is more and more likely to be not 'I' but 'the people who know what's good for me'.

The second thing we need to talk about is the way in which the people in charge pay us back, when we hand the power to decide our lives over to them.

And here an example may help.

Imagine, for a moment, that you are in a place called Jari Siya, in the remote and dusty north-west frontier region of Afghanistan, and that you are wearing the battle fatigues of an officer of the Norwegian army. Crouching down by the side of your armoured car, you can hear bullets whizzing past your head and pinging as they ricochet off the steel plate. You are here, since you ask, as part of a Nato force, and you've been involved in a fierce day-long firefight with around forty Taliban rebels. You and your men are pinned down; but at least you know that if you're hit, you can be quickly airlifted off by the German medical evacuation helicopters waiting behind the lines.

And then, all of a sudden, you hear the engines of those helicopters start up, and you look round to see them lifting off. As they gain height, you see them begin to turn away from where you are. At first you wonder what's going on – surely they can't be planning to leave you, under attack and without medical back-up? And then you look at your watch and realize that this is exactly what's happening. And the reason for this, of course, is that it's nearly teatime, and the helicopters have to go home. Under health-and-safety regulations, you see, the pilots aren't allowed to fly after dark, because it might be dangerous; and so around teatime they need to be off, to get safely back to base in Mazar-e-Sharif before the sun goes down.

This, by the way, actually happened, and was reported in *The Times* and elsewhere in November 2000.[18]

There is a principle behind this little event that seems to be characteristic of what happens, time and time again, when politicians and rule-makers take over, and when they impose rules and laws in areas where individuals used to be able to make their own decisions. What matters most of all, it seems, is being seen to be doing something, and setting down procedures to be followed. The actual practical results of what happens when those procedures are followed in any particular case seem to come a very distant second; and the possibility that it might be better, in some circumstances, to do things in some other way not set down in the rules, seems to be far beyond the official imagination.

'So people might have died after the helicopters left?' the implication seems to be, 'Well, no matter: at least you followed the procedures.'

You may never have been in a firefight with Taliban guerrillas, but you may well have flown in an aeroplane. If you have, you will probably have experienced a similar approach to safety in the way the authorities handle airport security.

Going through the airport, you'll have noticed that you encounter rather more safety procedures before you can board your plane than you used to a few years ago. Whoever you are and wherever you're going, you have to queue up for ages to put your bags through a scanner – which you might have done in the past, even if the queues weren't quite so long or so slow – but these days you often have to take off your jacket, your belt and perhaps even your shoes, too, and put those through with your bags. A lot of airports insist that you take toothpaste and shampoo out of your luggage and put it into a clear plastic bag. They don't seem to do any special tests on the toothpaste and shampoo once they're in the bag, and it all still goes through the scanner in exactly the same way that it would if it were still in your luggage, but the act of placing it into the plastic bag seems to have some sort of security role. While your bags, shoes, toothpaste and so on are being checked, you have to walk through a metal-detector gate and sometimes, when you come out the other side, you have to stand with your arms and legs outstretched for a body-search. At some airports they even have little booths with special cameras to allow the customs officers to see what you look like without your clothes on.

The aim of all of this, apparently, is safety.

It's to make it harder for you to take weapons or bombs on board your plane in order to hijack it and crash it into a skyscraper, if that's what you have in mind, or to attempt to set off the explosives cunningly concealed in the soles of your shoes in order to blow yourself and your fellow-passengers to bits, or use eyebrow tweezers or nail clippers as deadly weapons, or something along those lines.

But if safety were really the overriding concern, rather than the need to be seen to be doing something and the need to follow the rules to the letter, then your whole journey through the airport would, most likely, have been a lot quicker and easier.

At one time the police and the customs people would have done what they call 'passenger profiling', which means they would have mainly been on the lookout for passengers who looked a bit shifty or who were behaving oddly, or who fitted the profile of the particular kinds of criminals or terrorists that they had in mind.

Nowadays, though, it makes no difference to the searchers and the scanners whether you're an elderly nun from County Galway on your way to Lourdes or a young mum from Cheltenham with a baby and toddler in tow, or whether you're part of a group of Midwestern Rotarians on a cultural sightseeing tour of Europe: the rules say that everyone has to have an equal chance of being checked.

Nor does it matter that, although your own liquids and pastes have been placed in a plastic bag and those over a certain size confiscated, people coming in from a number of other airports can still carry all the liquids they want, and can pass them to you once you're through the security scan. The rules have to be followed, and everyone has to be seen to be following them, and that's what matters.

You may wonder what life will be like in the future, if things carry on like this.

What will the world be like when anxiety spirals completely out of control; when personal responsibility is non-existent and when every single decision affecting every aspect of our personal safety is made for us by other people?

As it happens, some people are already living in such a world: they're called 'children'.

RAISING CHILDREN IN CAPTIVITY

In 1990, a distinguished social scientist by the name of Mayer Hillman published *One False Move*,[19] a report into modern childhood commissioned by the Policy Studies Institute. This report examined the lives of primary-school children, aged between eight and eleven, in five English schools, and then compared what he found with what life had been like for children at the same schools in 1970, a generation before.

What he found was that in the space of those twenty years, life had changed beyond all recognition. In the seventies, most children of that age were free to go out to play, to cycle in the street, to walk to school and back on their own and, in many cases, to catch buses on their own. By the nineties, most children were no longer trusted, or allowed, to do any of these things.

What Hillman called the 'home habitat' of a typical eight-year-old – the area in which they are able to travel unaccompanied – had shrunk, by 1990, to one-ninth of its former size.

It's not that their parents didn't realize what they were doing: three-quarters of them agreed that they had had much more freedom than they allowed their own children, but they felt – like 80 per cent of the general public, if you remember back a few pages – that the world had become a much more dangerous place on account of all the people out to get the little'uns. Mad drivers, potential abductors and gangs of feral teenagers seemed more serious threats to the parents of the nineties than they had to those of the seventies.

You can probably guess what has happened in the seventeen years since, but I'll tell you anyway: the fears have become worse and the freedom has become even more restricted.

There is a long-term study by the Children's Society,[20] the Good Childhood Enquiry, and amongst the things it has done, according to a BBC report in 2007, is to map out the world of a typical nine-year-old girl and how it has changed over the years. In 1970 that girl would have been free to wander 919 yards – just over half a mile or a ten-minute walk – from her front door. A bizarrely precise figure, I know, however you choose to express it. (The authors of the report used metric, but 840 metres doesn't sound any more memorable or commonsensical either.) You can imagine the mother standing in the street and yelling, 'Susan! I said nine hundred and nineteen yards, not nine hundred and twenty: get back in your boundary this instant!' I think the figure must be some sort of average. Anyway, by 1997 the distance had shrunk to 306 yards – a three-and-a-half minute walk. And by 2007 the boundary had moved to just outside the front gate, which is, in time terms, a no-minute walk.

At the same time, walking to school pretty much died out altogether. In 1970 eight out of ten primary-school children used to walk to school. In 2007 fewer than one in ten did – and they were probably the ones who lived across the road or whose dads were the school caretakers. Most children these days are driven to school, even if they live just round the corner.

As for going out to play, children today can pretty much forget it. Almost half of all parents – 43 per cent – think that children shouldn't be allowed out of the house on their own, for any reason at all, until they are fourteen years old. You'd think that perhaps the grandparents might put a word in, draw on the wisdom of age and experience and all that, tell the parents to ease up a bit, but it turns out that they're even more cautious than their offspring. One in five people over sixty thinks the thing to do is to keep the children indoors until they're at least sixteen! By which age, of course, they themselves would have been holding down a full-time job for about ten years, working up chimneys or in boot-blacking factories or whatever it was that children did in those days.

So what they do, these children nowadays, is they stay at home. They stay at home and they watch the television. Did you know, by the way, that eight out of ten children have their own televisions in their bedrooms?[21] Mind you, their parents also have televisions all over the place: in the kitchen, in the bedroom, everywhere. You can even buy a waterproof TV, from a company called Tilevision, that you can watch in the shower or the bath.

Not only do children have their own televisions, but more than half of them have their own DVD players or video recorders. Many of them even have satellite-TV subscriptions, too. Anyway, they watch television, these children, or they listen to music, or they play computer games, or they argue with each other and slam their bedroom doors and annoy their parents, or they send text-messages to their friends on their mobile phones. Sometimes they do go out, though: generally to organized sports classes or other worthwhile, 'improving' activities. These activities, of course, are properly supervised by trained adults who have, it goes without saying, gone through the necessary police vetting procedures and filled out the appropriate risk-assessment forms.

This isn't just a British eccentricity, either.

In 2004, the *Sydney Morning Herald* reported the results of a survey that showed how boys and girls in Australia and New Zealand are treated like pampered prisoners – cosseted, constrained and constantly nagged.

One Australian mother interviewed in the paper described how she let her ten-year-old son cycle to and from school – but followed him in the car. Another followed her two primary-school-age daughters on foot as they cycled up and down their suburban street. And as in Britain, the number of children walking to school in Australia and New Zealand has plummeted, while the numbers being driven have rocketed. Even by the age of eleven, according to the survey, only a quarter of Australasian children are trusted on buses – whereas most of their parents' generation were at that age.

At some point or other, though, children do have to leave the house, whether it's to go to school or whether it's because they've reached the age where you just can't keep them in any longer.

But today's anxious adults aren't going to give up without a fight, and with the aid of modern technology they are able to keep their children, as far as possible, in the most controlled, risk-free environment they can manage.

One recent invention is called the Walkodile. It's a sort of caterpillar-like thing made up of plastic segments with handles on, designed to be used on trips and outings where groups of children have to walk along a street. Rather than telling the children to walk in pairs, you tog them up in reflective safety belts and then make them each hold a handle on the Walkodile. This is meant to prevent them from suddenly diving into the path of an oncoming car.

Alternatively, if you have allowed your child to go out into the garden and you are worried that he or she might wander off or be abducted, you can now buy the Toddler Tag from Connect Software, which attaches to your child's clothes and lets out a loud beep if it crosses a set boundary.

For older children and teenagers there are more sophisticated tracking devices. One is known as a 'mobile phone' and it allows parents to call their offspring every twenty minutes or so to check where they are and who they are with and what they are doing. However, because children have been known to do something called 'lying', it's also possible to buy devices like the Personal Companion from Globalpoint Technologies. The size of a small mobile phone, it uses GPS technology to allow parents to track their children's movements on an electronic screen on their computer or mobile phone display – rather like the Marauder's Map in the Harry Potter books.

Every age, of course, has had its minority of obsessively overprotective parents, and you may think that these sorts of devices are just for those kinds of people, rather than the normal ones. This is where you'd be mistaken. In 2007 the school-uniform company Trutex decided to look into the idea of incorporating tracking devices into its uniforms. To see what the likely demand was, it commissioned a survey of 809 parents, and asked them what they thought. The level of interest surprised them: it wasn't just 'a couple' of parents, or 'twenty or thirty' or even 'a hundred or so' who wanted what Trutex were proposing: it was actually 477 of the 809 – a full 59 per cent – who were worried enough about what might be happening to their children during the day to think that putting an electronic tracking device in their uniform would be a good idea.[22]

On one level they do have a point, though, some of these parents. There is danger out there for children – as indeed there always has been. The main source of that danger, though, is less to do with increased traffic levels or weird strangers and more to do with the way that children naturally are, and the things they have always managed to get up to once adults' backs are turned.

You might want to cast your mind back a bit to your own childhood, and see if there's anything there that you did which, if you saw a child doing it today, would turn your blood cold.

I'll give you a few of my own, to start you off.

One day, when I was about twelve or thirteen, I was walking down the road with my friend when we both became aware of a powerful smell of gas. And also a sort of hissing sound. Poking around a little, we found the source of the noise and the smell: there was gas leaking from a small hole by a fence at the edge of the pavement. It just so happened that I had a box of matches in my pocket, and it struck me then that it would be a really good idea to see what would happen if I lit one of the matches and held it to the hole. I'll tell you what happens, to save you trouble just in case you find yourself in the same situation. The bloody thing blows up – that's what happens – and it sends a huge great jet of flame whoosh-ing upwards. And the skin on your hand sort of melts away and you have to go to hospital.

Actually, my mother still thinks that it was a spark from my shoe that did it. I haven't quite managed to tell her the truth about it yet. And while we're on the subject of what people's parents don't know, my wife's parents won't know, until they read this, that she used to climb on the roofs of the garages at the back of her house as a child.

What else? I used to live near a London Underground station, where the trains ran on electrified rails. There were two ways to get from one platform to the other. One was to use the pedestrian footbridge: this was the proper way. The other was to climb down from the platform, step carefully across two sets of rails and then clamber up the other side. My friends and I found the second way more to our liking. One day, three of us were halfway across when we heard a pinging sound at our feet. This was caused by high-voltage pulses being pumped along the tracks. Which was bad enough in itself: one touch and you'd be fried. But more than just announcing the arrival of the electricity, the pinging is a sure sign that a train is imminent. And it was: looking up we saw the thing bearing down on us, at speed, about twenty yards away. God knows how we did it, but we were over those tracks and up on the platform in two seconds flat.

More? A group of us used to cycle fairly regularly from Dagenham, where we lived, to play in Hainault forest, about eight miles away, taking in a busy stretch of the A12 on the way and being overtaken at regular intervals by heavy lorries. One day, as we explored the ruins of a big old house across the road from the forest gate, I came across an open manhole. It must have been about ten or twelve feet deep, this manhole, and it had iron rungs protruding from the sides. Rather than climbing down it, I had the idea, with another boy, of covering it over with cardboard and twigs to make a sort of man-trap. Then we decided who we would like to see fall down it, and how we would go about it. What we did was to drag over an abandoned ladder from the remains of the house's garage and put one end by the hole. Then we announced that we were going to have a 'ladder race'. We would pair up and run from a starting line to the ladder, which we would pick up and run around the house with, and the fastest pair would be the winners. I volunteered to be the timekeeper. My co-conspirator offered to take the front of the ladder for the first race, and our victim was picked to take the back end, right by the hole. 'Ready?' I shouted, 'Steady . . . Go!' and *whoom!* – straight on the trap he trod. Luckily for him, though, it was only with his front foot, and so he just did the splits, with one leg on the ground and the other down the hole, rather than, say, shooting straight down it and being battered unconscious or worse by the iron rungs and breaking both his legs at the bottom. So the result was we all collapsed with laughter so loud and prolonged that it hurt, and not, in that instance, a trip in a speeding ambulance to the hospital or mortuary. And I've even forgotten the boy's name, now; but if you're reading this, mate, I'm sorry. I really am. You think differently as a child.

There are other things, too: things I put in my mouth to see what they felt like on my tongue – a broken asbestos pipe and a strange white chalky stone that turned out to be a calcified dog-dropping, not to mention drinking from muddy streams – all sorts of stomach-turning and heart-stopping stupidity.

For a while I thought it was just me, but the more people I've spoken to, the more shocking stories of childhood lunacy I get, and often from the least likely people. There seems to be a bit of a thing with boys and explosions, particularly for the generation brought up in the Second World War. My father-in-law seems to have spent half of his school chemistry lessons making illicit explosives and looking for places to set them off. He also told me about an army transport aeroplane that crashed in the woods at Ralph's Ride, near Bracknell, and how he and a lot of the other local boys explored the wreckage – and the bodies – for things to play with. He came away with handfuls of cordite from explosive shells, which he spent the following days trying to detonate. Other boys, meanwhile, found that they could get bullets to fire by using hammers and nails in the school toilets.

Tracking gadgets in uniforms aren't even the half of it: if parents knew all of the things their children get up to if left to their own devices, then no child would ever have been allowed to set foot outside the front door since front doors were invented.

No matter how safe an environment grown-ups try to create for their children, children themselves always seem to find a way to make it dangerous. If you've ever read *The Adventures of Tom Sawyer* then you'll know that what the nineteenth-century world lacked in terms of motor traffic and food additives it more than made up for in terms of disused mine shafts and evil villains – and children have always managed to find them out.

This has always been so. But, somehow, despite their best efforts to maim or kill themselves, most of them have managed to survive.

The difference now, though, is that this generation of adults actually are keeping their children indoors, and actually are keeping them, as far as possible, from experiencing any risks whatsoever, let alone life-threatening ones. And it's not so much because childhood has become any more dangerous than it was before, or because children have become any more foolhardy than ever they were: it's because we've all become much more anxious.

*

So this is the modern world that we live in, and that our children bear the full impact of. We worry more and more about threats to our health and safety and at the same time we find it hard, or unpleasant, to take full responsibility for our own actions – it all seems too dangerous, and too serious to handle alone. Because of this, we hand over responsibility to the People Who Know What's Good for Us, the politicians and the 'experts' – and they, in turn, respond by setting down more and more rules and laws and guidelines for us to follow, to the extent that our freedom to make our own decisions and take our own risks grows smaller with every passing day. And for our children, life now is utterly different from the life we ourselves led when we were growing up. We were outdoor, free-range children; they are indoor, battery-reared children. They are pampered and protected, and showered with attention and material goods, yet at the same time they are denied even the smallest fraction of the freedom and autonomy that every child once had.

PART TWO

SAFETY IN THE HOME?

SAFETY IN THE HOME?

Children can be a bit of a pain sometimes. I know that I was, quite a lot of the time, and I'll dare say that you had your moments too. There's also been a fair amount written, just lately, about how large numbers of children have become used to getting their own way more or less all of the time, and have managed to persuade their parents that it is their inalienable human right to have a constant supply of designer clothing, mobile telephones and Chicken McNuggets 'n' fries with a large fizzy drink of choice, to go, and to stay up until God knows what time, night after night, watching unsuitable programmes on their own personal televisions or playing unsuitable video games on their own personal video-game things, or doing unsuitable things generally, or just *being* unsuitable. There's been a lot written, just lately, about what's come to be known as a generation of pampered 'Little Princes and Princesses' raised in a culture of instant gratification, and how they simply refuse to do anything that irks them or inconveniences them in any way. Like eating with a knife and fork, say, or having to share things with other people without having a tantrum, or saying 'please' and 'thank you'; that sort of stuff. All of this, according to the leaders of Britain's two biggest teachers' unions, can be a little trying in the classroom when children turn up at school expecting to be indulged the way they are at home. It can also, presumably, end up being more than a little trying for the children's parents a few years later, when they stop being quite so little and cute, and when there are teenage bedrooms to be tidied or monthly credit-card bills and mobile-phone bills to be paid.

But as much as adults moan about 'children today' and as much as our parents moaned about us, we do rather like our own children, most of us, and we don't, generally, want anything really bad to happen to them, like a sudden, violent death or anything of that kind. Since we like our children and since, these days, we imagine the world to be chock-full of wicked people lurking in the streets and parks waiting to snatch them away, we don't tend to let them go out to play on their own any more. After all, as everyone never tires of telling you, 'You can't be too careful, these days.'

But let us imagine, for a moment, that this is what you do want to happen. Imagine, for a moment, that you have been pushed to the point of no return by your offspring's lack of table manners, or are facing personal bankruptcy due to their insatiable demands for chocolate and toys, or that you have simply decided, after careful consideration, that you have one or more children surplus to requirements.

Suddenly an idea strikes you: you begin to realize that all of those abductors and child-snatchers we hear so much about may actually present an opportunity rather than a threat. All you'd need to do, it would seem, to be rid of your unwanted child, would be to give it its breakfast, open the front door, send it out, and then sit back and wait for the inevitable to happen.

How long do you imagine that would take? Let's have a look at the facts.

In Britain, there are around 12 million children under the age of sixteen.[23] Every year, according to Home Office figures, fifty to sixty of them are abducted by strangers; and of those fifty to sixty, two thirds – around forty – are recovered within twenty-four hours.[24] Which means that around twenty children a year are abducted by complete strangers and not recovered within twenty-four hours, although eventually most of them do get found, alive and well.

And very, very exceptionally, a child is abducted and either never found again or is found dead. This happens very rarely – so rarely, in fact, that most of us can name them all, these children, and have seen their pictures on the front pages of our newspapers, and seen their frantic parents on our television screens making desperate appeals for their safe return; and then we have followed the trials of the killers when they are eventually caught.

Let's work out the odds. In any one year, the average child – your child, say – stands a 0.0005 per cent chance of being abducted by a stranger, a 0.00016 per cent chance of not being recovered within twenty-four hours, and an infinitesimally small chance of never being recovered alive.

Or, to put it another way, it would take your child, left outside, 200,000 years to be abducted, 600,000 years to be abducted for more than twenty-four hours, and several million years to be murdered.

So sending young children out to play is probably not a very good strategy for people who want to be rid of them. In fact, if what you don't like about your child is its constant activity and incessant chatter, then sending it outside to play will only make things worse: according to pretty much all of the published research, allowing the under-tens to play outdoors unsupervised makes them healthier and more sociable. Which, if you were rather hoping for the speedy abduction that so many people worry so much about, might not be what you have in mind at all.

But if you're a normal sort of parent, and if you want to keep all of your children alive and in one piece, you might say that even a tiny, once-in-several-million-years risk is still a risk you'd rather not take – not when you can keep them safe at home.

Although, saying that, the home isn't that safe a place at all, as far as children are concerned. A large proportion of all child murders take place at home, and the majority of the killers are parents, relatives or family friends.

And nor is the home that safe a place, comparatively speaking, even with non-homicidal parents, from the point of view of the whole place going up in flames with the children in it: three children a day are badly injured by flames or smoke inhalation in the home, and one child dies of it every ten days.

So, they go out, and very rarely indeed, one child of the 12 million gets abducted and murdered. Or they stay in, where one child gets burnt to death every ten days.

Nor is the home a particularly safe place for adults, either. In fact, more accidents happen at home than any-where else.

Every year the US National Safety Council publishes data covering all of the major causes of death and injury to US citizens, and lists against them the odds of your falling victim to them, both in one year and over the course of a lifetime, if you live in the USA or a country like it. Some of the 'hazards' they list are very unlikely indeed to happen to you: you stand, should you be interested to know, a 1 in 2 million chance of being killed by fireworks during your lifetime, and a 1 in 4 million chance of being killed while riding in a tram or streetcar. You also stand, slightly more worryingly, a 1 in 140,000 chance of being killed by a dog: twenty-seven Americans went that way in 2004.[25]

But of particular interest here are the figures relating to accidents and injuries in the home. Did you know, for example, that in any one year, you have a 1 in 36 chance of being disabled for a day or more due to an accident in your house or flat? This is a far greater risk than for work and motor accidents combined.

Being disabled for a day or more is unpleasant, but it gets worse: the home can kill you, too. Particularly if it has stairs in it. According to Professor Richard Wilson of Harvard University, falls kill 16,000 Americans every year. And then you have all the other potential causes of death indoors: the drilling into power cables, the accidental electrocutions from faulty appliances, the fires and the gas explosions and so on.

Even if you've managed to negotiate the stairs without killing yourself, staying in bed isn't hazard-free. In any one year, NSC statistics show that you have a 1 in 650 chance of being injured by your bed, your mattress or your pillow.[26] You could even die from it: in 2004, nearly 800 Americans were killed falling out of or over beds or other soft furnishings. And you'd have to get out of bed at some point, if only to go to the bathroom, where you will have a 1 in 4,500 chance of being injured by your toilet. Have a shave and you stand a 1 in 7,000 chance of needing medical attention for razor cuts.

You could try to get out, just a little – maybe out into the garden, say. But if you were to do that, it is only fair that you should know that according to Britain's Royal Society for the Prevention of Accidents,[27] 300,000 people are injured in their gardens every year – over a third of them seriously enough to need hospital treatment. The risks include:

Lawnmowers (6,500 accidents in Britain each year)
Flower pots (5,300)
Secateurs (4,400)
Spades (3,600)
Electric hedge trimmers (3,100)
Plant tubs and troughs (2,800)
Shears (2,100)

Garden forks (2,000)

Hoses and sprinklers (1,900)

Garden canes and sticks (1,800)

I would have thought that rakes might have appeared somewhere in the list, but maybe people are acutely aware of the risks involved in stepping on one end, and the handle flying up and smacking you in the face, having seen that particular thing happen so much in television comedies.

But all of these risks are dwarfed by the biggest garden risk of all, which is the fall – either just falling over generally, or from a step-ladder or other contraption. That injures 110,000 people in Britain alone every year.

But assuming that you do stay at home, and venture no further than your garden, and assuming that you manage to avoid being injured by your bed, your toilet, your stairs or your razor in your home, and the perils of the flower-pot in your garden, there are the inescapable, creeping effects on your physical and mental health of staying at home all day, every day, for any length of time – less spectacular, perhaps, than a faulty electric socket or a headlong tumble down the stairs, or tripping on a hose and falling head-first into a plant tub or trough, but no less serious for that: the depression, the weight gain, the muscle wastage, the increased risk of heart disease, the decreased life expectancy, the sheer crushing awfulness of it. The sort of life, in fact, which even if it didn't actively kill you outright, would begin to make out-of-control alcoholism look like an attractive alternative.

You'd actually be a lot safer and a damn sight happier running off to join the circus and taking a job as a lion tamer or a trapeze artist.

THE POISONS ON YOUR PLATE

Whether you decide to go out of your house, or whether you decide to stay indoors, there are a number of dangers that are very hard to avoid.

One of them is money. Other people have touched it, you see, and you don't know, and can't control, where they've been putting it or what else they've been touching. It is a fact that a full half of all coins and banknotes carry infectious germs. You could, at a push, avoid direct contact with money, by using tongs or rubber gloves and plenty of disinfectant, but to do that you'd need to be prepared to live a life of Howard Hughes-style bonkersness and, probably, to spend most of your life indoors. As discussed previously.

Even harder to avoid than money are air and food, both of which can be surprisingly bad for you.

The air we breathe contains molecules of some of the world's most deadly poisons, including dioxin, arsenic, mercury and benzene – particularly in towns and cities. In

America, polluted urban air has been estimated to kill some 20,000 people a year on the East Coast alone.[28] And as for food, well, we'll come to that in just a moment.

You could try to avoid air, of course, like some super-rich eccentrics who install oxygen chambers in their homes to save them from having to breathe the same air as everyone else, but this won't improve your social life.

You can even try to avoid food. A couple of years back there was a New Age 'guru' in Australia who went by the name of Jasmuheen. I don't know if that was her actual name, or whether she was really called something like Marjoreen or Vassaline or Doris or Sheila, but whatever her real name was, Jasmuheen claimed that she had transcended the need to eat food like normal people. Instead, she got all the nourishment she needed from the 'prana', or spiritual energy, found in pure sunlight. She wrote best-selling books to that effect, and a surprising number of people believed them. When journalists photographed her and her husband shopping for regular human food in a supermarket and taking it back to their house, she insisted that she never touched the stuff. When the televised 'experiment' in which she was challenged to demonstrate under controlled conditions that she didn't eat ended because she became dangerously emaciated, she blamed the producers for putting her beside a busy main road. 'I asked for fresh air. Seventy per cent of my nutrients come from fresh air. I couldn't even breathe.' And still people believed her. Worse than that, some other 'breatharians', as they're known, tried to live on prana too, and what happened to the ones who took it all the way was the same as what happens to everyone who stops eating, whether they've got 'fat genes' or not: they wasted away and they died.[29]

All of which goes to show that unless you really can survive on sunlight alone, you're going to have to accept the risks involved in eating food.

People get quite worked up about food – what's good for you and what's not, how much fat it's safe or healthy to eat and of what kind, the role of protein and carbohydrates – and it all gets rather complicated and confusing, particularly when even the experts seem to disagree with each other, and when the official advice on what's safe and what's healthy changes from year to year. One moment you're feeling all virtuous for giving your family low-fat everything and skimmed milk that tastes like white-coloured water and low-calorie margarine, or Marjoreen, that's about as enjoyable and as satisfying as prana, and the next minute it turns out that you're giving them malnutrition, as well as taking all the pleasure out of life, and they need a bit of fat inside them. Then, just as you're filling your shopping-basket with polyunsaturates, word comes through that you now have to get monounsaturates. So you dump all of your first basket on the nearest shelf, so giving the supermarket's latest graduate intake of shelf-stackers the task of putting them all back where they belong, while you rush round seeking out the stuff you're meant to have. You queue up behind fifteen people at the checkout, but just as you eventually get to the front there's an announcement over the tannoy: 'Here is the latest Food Fad Alert: Monounsaturates are old hat. Please buy only products containing Omega-3.' And so it goes on.

It would take a whole book to go into the ins and outs of food, but one thing that worries people a lot, and that touches particularly on the theme of this book, is pesticides and poisons. These are now popularly known as toxins by the people who are most concerned about them, in the same way that jogging is now known as running, which is what it used to be called before it was called jogging. But toxins are a big concern – especially pesticides, which are, after all, designed to kill living creatures.

The feeling generally is that you're better off not having pesticide residue on your food, all things considered, on account of it turning your children into mutants.

For this reason people fork out extraordinary amounts of money for 'organic' food (as opposed to what? Inorganic? Mineral?), which is grown, as far as is possible, without using synthetic pesticides. Now, there are a number of very good reasons why organic farming is a good idea. In particular, the countryside looks much prettier and teems with far more life without regular dousings of Agent Orange or whatever it is that industrial farmers use to kill off anything that doesn't make a profit.

However, having organic food on your plate doesn't stop you eating pesticides. The only thing that stops you eating pesticides is stopping eating food.

You see, as a result of an 'evolutionary arms-race' between the world's plants and the various caterpillars and mites and grazing creatures that want to eat them, almost all plants in the world today contain chemicals which poison or otherwise deter unwanted parasites. These are what you might call naturally occurring pesticides.

According to Bruce Ames, Professor of Biochemistry and Molecular Biology at the University of California at Berkeley, 99.9 per cent of the pesticides in our diet are chemicals that plants produce naturally. The average person eats between five and ten thousand different kinds of natural pesticides in a lifetime, and whether you pay more for 'organic' or whether you don't makes little difference.[30]

Just in case you think I'm quibbling with words here, and using 'pesticide' to cover both natural chemicals (good) which are nutritious to humans and synthetic chemicals (bad) which make your children glow in the dark or grow an extra head, consider this: of the forty-seven different naturally occurring pesticide compounds that have been isolated from plants so far, more than half have been shown to cause cancer in animals. The amount of cancer-inducing chemicals in food from artificial pesticides pales besides what's already there in nature.

A couple of examples for you: roast coffee, whether organic, fair-trade or otherwise, contains a thousand chemicals. Of the twenty-six that have been tested, nineteen have been shown to cause cancer in rats. And naturally occurring compounds in mushrooms (hydrazine), spices (safrole), parsley (psoralen) and bread (ethyl carbamate) have all caused cancers in laboratory animals.[31]

And quite apart from the pesticides, there are the poisonous compounds you create when you cook food. Burnt toast, for example (and, for that matter, barbecued or smoked meats), contains benzopyrene, while potato crisps and fried carbohydrate foods contain acrylamide – both of which are recognized causes of cancer. In fact, according to Professor Ames, the toxins found in the amount of cooked food eaten by one person in an average day are several hundred times more carcinogenic than severe air pollution.

To this you can add the fact that all substances – including the healthiest, most nutritious foods and drinks – can kill you if you have too much of them. Even pure natural water: drink more than two gallons of it at once and you'll die of water poisoning, a fate which has befallen a number of young people seeking to negate the potentially harmful effects of dancing for too long under the influence of the chemical toxin known as Ecstasy: drink plenty of water, the advice goes. Yes, well, perhaps not quite so much, eh? Two and a half pounds of sugar will kill you, too, as will seven ounces of salt, or the caffeine in a hundred cups of coffee – although you can overdose and need to be rushed to hospital to have your stomach pumped out after considerably less, as seventeen-year-old Jasmine Willis found out in 2007 when she drank just seven double espressos.[32] Even simple, honest-to-goodness organic vegetables can prove fatal: ten pounds or so of spinach, for example, contains enough oxalic acid to leave you good only to be used as organic fertilizer.

Knowing all this, you might want to give fruit and vegetables and cooked food a miss, and maybe live on something like pure natural yoghurt. Which, if you are a woman, may increase your chance of getting ovarian cancer, according to some studies

So on the basis that no one can live entirely free from risk, and even if you never venture outdoors and eat only the purest, simplest, most naturally grown foods in the world you will still be exposed to at least as many dangers as anyone else, let's take a look at some of the other fears that bother us these days, and see how well-grounded or otherwise they really are.

THE RISKS OUTSIDE YOUR FRONT DOOR

If you want to live anything like a normal life, you need to get out and about a bit. For most short distances you can get by with walking, but if you want to go more than a few miles from where you live, and if you have neither the time nor the inclination to make all of your long journeys on foot, then you'll probably end up taking some sort of motorized transport.

One form of motorized transport that gets a lot of people worried is the aeroplane. Specifically, aeroplanes crashing, either through mechanical failure or pilot error or, more recently, fundamentalist nutters barricading themselves into the cockpit and setting course for the nearest tall building. Which could happen. Which has happened, in fact, as we've all seen on the television and read about in the newspapers. But it just doesn't happen very often, and it's very, very unlikely to happen to you, no matter how many times you fly.

Let's look at this another way. Imagine that you're fed

up with life and you want to die, but you're too scared to do any of the things that people usually do when they kill themselves, like diving under a train or swallowing a bucketload of pills. Let's imagine, instead, that you'd rather go in a plane crash, strapped into a comfortable(ish) economy-class seat with a mixed-sandwich medley, a small packet of baked nut-free crunchy snacks and a plastic cup of coffee on your tray to ease your way, and a planeload of fellow-travellers to keep you company. You've saved up a bit of money for your plane tickets, and got some time off of work, and so you set about your task, resolving to book yourself an airline ticket every day, until you strike it lucky.

How long will that take you, do you think?

I'll tell you how long: assuming that you had all the money and the time you needed, you'd have to take a flight a day, every single day, for 26,000 years to be sure of crashing.[33]

But by then, if you'd made your way to the airport by car – and assuming that was the only driving you did – the odds are that you would already have been killed more than twenty times over on the roads. And if as well as driving to and from the airport you'd been using a car for the other typical, everyday things that people use them for as well, then you'd end up being killed more than 180 times on the roads before you managed to board your fatal flight.

People worry about planes nevertheless. Around 10 million people in Britain suffer from some form of fear of flying.[34] This is many, many times more than the number of people who are scared of getting into a car.

Cars, as it happens, are very dangerous things indeed. They kill, around the world, 3,000 people every day. That's pretty much the same as the total number of people who died in the worst-ever aeroplane-related disaster, the September 11 attacks in New York, and it happens every single day of the year. For some reason, though, cars don't seem to arouse nearly so much panic.

It's not so much that any one trip in a car is particularly dangerous: on any average journey, the odds against you crashing and dying are around 4 million to 1 – or to put it another way, half as likely as your being struck by lightning at some point in your life. What makes it so particularly risky is the number of times we take this risk in the course of our lifetimes. This brings the odds right down. For the average person, taking the average number of car journeys, your chance of being killed in a car crash in any one year is around 140 to 1. Or, to put it another way, if you were born blessed with perfect health and eternal youth, but you travelled by road, you'd most likely still end up dead in a car crash before the age of 140.[35]

Of course we've been talking about averages here, and the average risks of crashing and dying. But average risks are made up of high and low risks, and there are things you can do to lower your risk of being killed. Not driving like a bloody maniac is one of them, of course, and goes without saying. Avoiding driving between 11 p.m. and 5 a.m. is another: over a third of all fatal crashes happen then, despite the fact that only 5 per cent of all journeys take place during those hours. And particularly avoid driving after midnight on Fridays and Saturdays: if you do that, you'll cut your risk of a fatal accident by 20 per cent.[36]

If you absolutely have to travel at dangerous times or on dangerous roads where you're more likely to have a crash, the best thing you can do to stay alive is to buy a car that's bigger and heavier than most of the others on the road: in a smash between two vehicles of different sizes, the driver of the smaller one is seventeen times more likely to die than the driver of the bigger.[37]

Another way to travel is by bicycle. In terms of what happens in the event of a crash between a car and a bike, it's like the big car/small car principle, only more so. Generally, you'll get flattened, while the car driver might feel a bit of a nasty bump as his wheels go over you. For now, all I'll say is that people who commute by bicycle are eleven times more likely to be killed in a crash than people who commute by car.[38] However, hold that thought, because there are a number of other complicating factors involved in this bike versus car thing, and – as we'll see a little later in this book – if you look deeply into the question 'Is it safer to ride a bike or to drive a car?' the answer isn't necessarily what you might think, even with the 'eleven times more likely to die in a crash' factor. But that's for later.

For now, let's just say that more people are scared of getting onto planes, which are unlikely to kill you, than are scared of getting into cars, which are a lot more likely to kill you.

Which is to say, the things that frighten us and the things that might kill us aren't always the same.

That's quite a striking thought, and one that bears looking at a little more closely. Let's start with an activity that's generally thought of as dangerous, even by the people who do it: smoking. Now, there are all sorts of facts and figures about the health risks of cigarettes – like the fact that each cigarette takes, on average, ten minutes to smoke and takes five minutes off of your life expectancy – but the one statistic I want to look at here is one that came from a famous study by the American scientist Richard Wilson, which was published in the journal *Technology Review* back in 1979.[39] The statistic is this: smoking 1.4 cigarettes increases your risk of dying by 1 in a million. In itself, that doesn't mean too much – we don't tend to think in terms of 'one-in-a-million' risks – but what it does, though, and what Wilson did in his paper, is provide a standard against which to judge the risk of a whole range of other activities. The findings are genuinely surprising, and challenge our comfortable certainties about what is and isn't risky. In fact, why not have a go yourself? Below are six different activities from Wilson's list, all of which increase your risk of death to a greater or lesser degree. See if you can rank them in order of danger, with the most risky at the top and the least risky at the bottom.

— 2 months in a brick-built house
— 6 minutes in a canoe
— 300 miles in a car
— 1 chest X-ray
— 40 tablespoons of peanut butter
— Living 5 years outdoors at the site boundary of a nuclear power plant

Done it?

Congratulations: you got the order right.

Whatever order you put them in, you got the order right, because they're all equally dangerous, and all as dangerous as smoking 1.4 cigarettes.

The risk of dying in an accident in six minutes in a canoe is as great as the risk of crashing while driving 300 miles in a car, which, in turn, is the same as the risk of contracting cancer from a substance known as aflatoxin-B, which comes from a mould that grows on poorly stored peanuts; and these risks are the same as that of contracting cancer from the radiation involved in a chest X-ray. And to be exposed to the same amount of radiation from being near a nuclear power plant, you'd have to stay outdoors right at the perimeter fence for five years. Meanwhile, if you stayed indoors for two months, miles and miles away from any power stations or X-ray machines, you'd still be exposed to a similar level of radiation, emitted from the bricks in your walls.

Some of those things may have surprised you. My guess is that you wouldn't have put living for years in the open air at the boundary of a nuclear power plant on a level with eating peanut butter or living for a couple of months in a normal brick house; but those are the facts, and they just go to show how wrong we can be.

If 'an increased risk of one in a million' is a bit abstract for you, and if peanut-butter poisoning seems a bit far-fetched for you to worry about, another way of looking at risk is by asking how many times you'd need to do a thing before it ends up killing you. Here are some examples from the UK Health and Safety Executive in 2007:[40]

Childbirth	1 death in 8,200 maternities
Hang-gliding	1 death in 116,000 flights
Surgical anaesthesia	1 death in 185,000 operations
Scuba-diving	1 death in 200,000 dives
Rock climbing	1 death in 320,000 climbs
Canoeing	1 death in 750,000 outings
Rail travel	1 death in 43,000,000 passenger journeys
Aircraft accidents	1 death in 125,000,000 passenger journeys
Fairground rides	1 death in 834,000,000 rides

That's probably enough lists for now. The more you see of them, though, the more you realize just how wrong your own judgement of risk can be. You probably wouldn't have thought, for example, that having a baby could be 39 times more dangerous than rock climbing, or that it could be 15,000 times more dangerous than flying, but it is.

So now is probably a good time to look at why there's often such a difference between the things that scare us and the things that actually kill us.

THE THINGS THAT SCARE US MOST

I have two stories for you, about two deaths. Not the cheeriest of subjects, but death comes to us all. And the fear of death, and the things that might cause it, is with us much of the time. I want to use these two stories to make a point about why some things scare us more than others.

The first story is about my father, and how he died.

My father had cancer of the bladder. He had it operated on, but it came back and grew and it spread, and, one day, after he'd set off in his car for a seaside town some miles away from where he lived for no reason that he could explain, they did a scan on his head, and discovered that there were secondary tumours in his brain. There was nothing that could be done about them. He was going to die. He knew that: we all knew. We talked about it, made jokes about it at times, but underneath it all there was a kind of strange anticipation, a wondering when it would

78

be and how it would be and what it would be like. He wanted to stay at home for as long as possible, but it became hard for him just getting out of bed, and after a while he had to be supported under the shoulders and helped to walk across to the lavatory next to the down-stairs room where his bed had been set up. He was much lighter than he had once been, lighter and more frail.

From time to time, they took him into hospital for treatment to ease the pain. He had times when things seemed to stabilize, and during those times he went back home again. And it happened, one day, that he reached one of his stable times, and it was arranged that he would leave hospital for a couple of months. A day or so before he was due to leave, I was at work when there came a telephone call from my brother. 'You need to come now,' he said, 'if you want to see Dad alive.' I left work, got the train, took a taxi to the hospital and was shown through to the ward where a curtain had been drawn around his bed. He was there, inside, flat on his back, unconscious, eyes closed, and all of what was still there of him seemed to be turned inwards, fighting to breathe. He would breathe in, long and slow and laboured, and then nothing, and then the out-breath would come. And then nothing. One second. Two seconds. Three seconds. Four. Five. Six. And on, and on. And then, slowly, slowly, the struggle to breathe in again. And this went on for hours. At least, I think it was hours: you lose track of time at times like this. Outside the curtain, in the next bed, listening, was a fellow patient. 'He's dying, too,' my dad had said, introducing him to me a few weeks before. 'We all are, in here.'

The doctors said, 'You can speak to him. He's still there. He can hear you.' They said that, but I don't think that he could. I think the doctors just said that to allow me what they call 'closure', to say things I had always meant to say, but hadn't. But what do I know?

And then came the breath that was followed by no more. And that was it.

Did I say his eyes were closed when I arrived?

Maybe they were. But maybe they weren't, because I remember his eyes being open, when he was dead, and trying to close them, and they wouldn't close.

The second story is about the death – or what I'm pretty sure was the death – of someone else's father.

He was in his sixties, I would guess. Thick-set. Olive-skinned. Middle-Eastern in origin, I imagine. His daughter was with him. She was in early middle age, although I can't picture her so clearly now. And she was standing, looking down at him where he lay, as a crowd gathered around them both. The car that had hit him – well, it was more than a car, really, it was what they call a people-carrier, halfway in size between a car and a mini-bus – was dark blue, and marked with the livery of a private-hire taxi company, and it stood with its nose sticking out into Oxford Street, and the driver sat in it.

He was on his back, the man, and utterly still. I checked, but could not feel a pulse or see any signs of breathing. There were bubbles of thick dark-red blood on his lips. 'We shouldn't try to move him,' I said, 'in case he's broken his neck,' and then I thought of him choking on his own blood, and that maybe he ought to be on his side, in the recovery position, and I started to push him but he was like a lead weight; and I thought about his neck again, and left him as he was. And I called for an ambulance on my mobile phone at some point. And when the ambulance had come I walked away, and began to make my way back to work when, quite suddenly, I felt faint and sick and had to sit down, right there and then, on a doorstep, with my head in my hands.

Two stories. Two deaths. One by disease and one by accident.

And I'd like to ask you a question about death, and the causes of death. It is a question which comes in two parts.

The first part is this: which kills more people – accident or disease?

Think about it a bit, and decide which you think is the right answer – and there is a right answer to this.

Now here's the second part: whichever cause of death you consider to be the biggest killer, whether you chose accident or disease, how many times more people do you think it kills than the other cause, the one you think kills fewer people?

When you've done that, have a look at the answer, which is printed in small letters at the bottom of the page.*

Did that surprise you?

The chances are that it did. Most people get it wrong.

I'm not just saying that because I got it wrong, or because I asked a handful of my friends, and most of them got it wrong: I'm saying it because it's been proven over and over again in an experiment designed by two psychologists by the name of Slovic and Fischhoff, and since replicated, with exactly the same results, in universities all over the world.

In experiments, most people either pick the wrong

* Disease kills fifteen times more people than accident worldwide.

82

cause of death altogether as the biggest killer, or else they imagine that the difference between the two causes is much smaller than it actually is.

For some reason it just feels, to most of us, that the other cause, the one that kills fifteen times fewer people, is a lot more important than it actually is, and many of us worry much more about it.

But if you look at the list below, taken from the UK Health and Safety Executive's 2007 report, which compares the annual risk of death from one of the big killer diseases with a range of accidental causes, you'll see how dramatic the difference is between them:

Cancer	1 in 387
Injury/poisoning	1 in 3,137
Road accidents	1 in 16,800
Gas incident	1 in 1,510,000
Lightning	1 in 18,700,000

It makes you wonder why that should be so. It makes you wonder why, with all of us inhabiting a world in which people die, and many of us having known, or at least heard of, people who've died over the course of our lives, we should get a simple question of everyday fact like that so very wrong? Why do we overestimate the risk of accident so dramatically and underestimate the risk of disease?

As I say, I've witnessed both kinds of death, and what I can say from my own experience is that, while an expected death leaves you feeling empty and bereft, a sudden death actively shocks you, both in the emotional and the medical sense of the word: you may feel weak, you may feel dizzy and you may feel nauseous. It isn't only TV policemen who throw up at the sight of a dead body.

And here's the thing: it is the power of an event to cause such emotional upheaval that matters most when it comes to the way we judge and rate risks and dangers. A classic study, carried out by Slovic, Fischhoff and three of their colleagues in the early 1980s,[41] established that it's the presence of 'outrage factors' – things that get you emotionally worked up – that makes certain things 'disproportionately visible', so that you notice them more and assign to them higher probability of risk. And it's this quality, rather than any rational calculation of statistical risk, that gives you the particular set of worries and fears that you have.

Which is why, when 3,000 people die on a single day in a spectacular terrorist attack in New York, you never hear the end of it: you get television programmes and candlelit vigils and all sorts. And it's also why, when a similar number of people die every single day on the world's roads, just as they've done every day since cars were invented, or when many millions more die of familiar diseases, you never hear the beginning of it.

That's not to say that people don't get worked up about diseases. They do. They just don't get worked up about the diseases they ought to, if they were approaching the world rationally. It's new, rare and unfamiliar diseases that worry people the most, particularly ones with sudden and shocking ways of killing you. Every few years, in fact, people work themselves up into a major panic about the latest 'novelty disease': things like mad-cow disease, salmonella in eggs and bird flu. If I remember rightly, mad-cow disease killed about five people, salmonella in eggs killed more or less no one and, as for bird flu, if you want to get it you have to live in an infected hen coop for about ninety years, as far as I can work out, and drink chickens' blood for breakfast every day.

But I'm still waiting for the panic caused by the fact that a third of us – yes, one in every three – will die from heart disease. And that's a fact. It just doesn't strike us as a particularly horrid, strange, wicked or unfair one. It doesn't get us worked up. It doesn't have dispropor-tionate emotional visibility, and so we don't develop the same sorts of fears about it.

An example for you of how serious risks get ignored and how less serious ones make people scared, because of disproportionate emotional visibility: in the late 1990s the inhabitants of the state of New Jersey were warned that a cancer-inducing, radioactive substance was widespread in homes throughout the state, threatening the health of thousands of residents. You'd imagine that if anything was going to cause people to worry, it would be something like that, and State officials were in two minds about even publicizing the information, in case it set up a panic. But in the event they met with the opposite problem – when they told people what the danger was, no one seemed to care.[42]

There was a reason for this: the cancer-causing radioactive substance in question was radon gas, which is something that occurs naturally in pretty much all of the rocks and soils of the state, and always had done. It's silent, invisible, unnoticed and natural, and generations have grown up with radon gas in their homes, and have lived and died without ever having being aware of its presence. That's not to say that people haven't been killed by it: it's just that if they have, the rest of the population seem not to have noticed the fact. This natural radon didn't force itself onto their consciousness or churn up their emotions. It didn't have disproportionate emotional visibility, and so everyone ignored it.

Compare and contrast this with what happened a few

years later, when state officials tried to use an abandoned quarry in rural New Jersey to dispose of soil containing radon-emitting industrial waste from an old luminous-paint factory. Now, the concentration of radon in this waste wasn't very high at all: it was far lower, in fact, than the radon occurring naturally throughout the state. On top of this, the quarry was miles from the nearest town, and so the officials didn't think anyone would be particularly bothered. They were wrong. There was a difference with this radon, as far as local people were concerned. It wasn't 'natural', you see: it came from some weird chemical stuff cooked up in a factory. More than this, it wasn't just there, in the quarry, of its own accord: someone had tried to put it there, on purpose, and they hadn't asked the local community for its permission to do so, or even told them what was being done.

So what happened? What happened was that people were up in arms, and angry citizens formed committees, painted banners, organized petitions and demonstrations and even threatened civil disobedience – and eventually the plan was blocked. Which may have been a good thing; but meanwhile these same people continued to ignore the far worse radioactivity that was seeping into their own homes every day from the rocks and soil all around them.

That's what we do, all of us: we irrationally overestimate the dangers of the strange, the shocking, the disproportionately visible. We worry too much about the things that grab our attention and churn up our emotions; and we don't worry nearly enough about the quieter but equally real dangers that lie unremarked in the familiar things of life.

So we ought to spend a little bit of time looking at *why* we do this. And to do so we need to understand how our brains are built, and how they work in relation to risk and fear. This will help us sort out which things and which behaviours we can change at will, should we want to do so. It will also help us to see which things are physically built into us – 'hard-wired' into us, to use the modern phrase – which we can never change, and which we just have to learn to live with as best we can.

PART THREE

DANGER ON THE BRAIN

HOW TO FRIGHTEN YOURSELF

Here's something for you to try, if you're reasonably brave or reasonably stupid, and if you want to understand how fear works.

It involves using an arrow. You can buy an arrow from an archery shop, I'd imagine, if there is such a thing. Otherwise try the Internet: it's amazing what you can get on it these days. You don't need anything fancy, no titanium or carbon-fibre, no razor-sharp big-game tips: just a regular 'bullet-tipped' wooden arrow of the kind that archers use for target practice, the ones that they shoot at those big packed-straw targets.

As well as your arrow, you'll need a friend with a steady hand.

Once you've got your arrow and your friend, you might want to get some idea of what you're letting yourself in for beforehand: if you whack the arrow against your hand, or your friend's, you will see how solid is, and if you can somehow manage to have a go at shooting it from a bow, you will see how far it can penetrate a target, if you hit it.

It's a fairly serious thing.

Once you've done all that, if you're still game, it's time to get on to the important part, the part that will help you to understand your own fear a little bit better.

What you need to do for this is to stand facing your friend, with a few feet between you. He or she should hold the arrow by the feathered end and push the metal tip lightly into the hollow in your throat, just above your breastbone. Adjust your distance so that your friend is standing with legs braced and arms outstretched, and you can feel the slightly uncomfortable pressure of the metal point pushing into your throat.

Next clasp your hands behind your back, take one deep breath and walk forward, decisively, onto the point of the arrow, leaning into it with all your body-weight.

What will happen when you do this is that the arrow will snap. It will snap surprisingly easily, and you will be completely unharmed.

The difficult part is actually getting yourself to do it, even when you know that this is what will happen. It can be explained to you really clearly and persuasively, and you can be completely convinced by the explanation and yet most people still find that actually doing it, in real life, is another matter altogether.

You will stand there, your heart will pump, your palms will sweat, you will tell yourself that you will be all right, and yet the chances are that you won't move.

You will be transfixed by a sort of inner turmoil, which will, eventually, resolve itself in one of two ways. Either you will step back, smile and say, 'No. Not today, thank you. Not now. Not for me,' or else you'll keep egging yourself on, winding yourself up to do it until all of a sudden you will feel a sudden rush of energy and a sense of letting go, and a voice in your head telling you, 'Yes. Now. Do it.' And then you'll step forward and the arrow will snap like matchwood, and you'll be astounded that it was so easy, and feel elated at what you've done, and you'll wonder why you made such a fuss, and wonder what it was that kept you from doing it when you knew all along that there was nothing to worry about.

Actually, you don't have to do this experiment. In fact, I'd rather you didn't, particularly if you use the wrong sort of arrow or something, or have unusually thin skin, and end up killing yourself by some complete fluke, and, more to the point, if your grieving relatives end up suing me for everything I've got. So don't.

A less fraught alternative is to think back to the times

in your life where you've been in a similar sort of turmoil over something that seemed equally risky or daunting.

The first time your dad took the stabilizers off of your bike, perhaps, and put you on board and started you off, and said, 'Ready now?' Or younger still, when your parents tried to get you to eat something 'grown-up' that you'd never tried before, but which you imagined that you would find revolting. And perhaps they patiently (or less patiently) explained how lovely it was, and how other children your age all found it delicious, and invited you to watch how – *Yum! We like this!* – it tasted absolutely delicious, and rather like your current favourite food – *Look, I'm not going to stand here all day holding this fork. Just open up and pop it in. It's simple. No need to cry about it. Just try. It's really nice. Honestly it is* – and for a moment you allowed yourself to be persuaded, and thought that perhaps it might be nice, and then the fork came nearer and you felt yourself start to gag . . .

What I'm getting at here is this: how you judge danger, and how you react in the face of it, involves much more than just your thinking mind. Your thinking mind may well be part of it, but it's a much smaller and much less powerful part than you may think. There's something else involved as well, a second party living inside you, something deeper and stronger and altogether more animal, something that is capable not just of overriding your conscious decisions, but of reducing you to a quivering wreck while it's at it.

'I will walk onto this arrow,' you may think. 'I know it's perfectly safe, just like the nice man in the book told me,' but if this other thing deep inside your mind decides otherwise, if this other thing decides you're not doing it, then you're not doing it.

It's like standing at the top of the high-diving board looking down, or like trying to pick up a spider when you've had a crippling phobia about them since childhood: you can argue with yourself all you like, and tell yourself how foolish you're being, and how you'd be perfectly all right if you just let go and did it, but if the decision's been made elsewhere, you ain't going nowhere.

I'll tell you more about what it feels like for me, and you can see if that's what it feels like for you, too, or whether you feel a different way. Here's what I feel: at times of crisis, at times of overwhelming physical fear, at times when one part of me desperately wants to do something that the other part wants to run a mile from, it feels to me as if there are two absolutely separate creatures, both living inside my skin, both looking out of my eyes and feeling the wind on my face.

One is utterly cerebral and logical, but not very good

when it comes to action: I imagine a dry and rather ineffectual old professor, sitting in his study, rather good at calculating what ought to be done, in theory. And then there's the other, his companion, all flesh and blood and powerful emotion: I picture a huge dog, immensely strong but very easily spooked. Most of the time they rub along well enough together, these two, and most of the time you aren't aware of any difference between them, or of any disagreement between them. Which makes sense, since they are both concerned with the same end, which is to save the body they inhabit from the dangers it faces. But they have different approaches and different ways of going about things, and different ways of judging what is dangerous and what isn't; and occasionally, at times of greatest stress and fear, one of them will want to go off in one direction while the other will want to go a different way; and that's when you really start to feel what's going on inside your mind.

There are times when the professor can get the dog to go along with what he wants, with a little bit of encouragement and cajoling, but it depends always on the dog giving consent. When it comes to a straight battle of wills – as with walking onto an arrow or diving from the high board or picking up the spider or any of the many other things that can paralyse us with fear, despite ourselves – when it comes to these things, and when the dog absolutely refuses to budge, the professor is helpless.

I do wonder sometimes if the reason human beings have always got on so well with real dogs is because we have so much in common, in the way we feel and in the way we act. Strip away the human capacity for fancy abstract thought and there's not a great deal to choose between us, I sometimes think. We are old companions: we understand each other; we have sympathy for each other.

Or perhaps not: it's just an analogy, after all. But there being two competing parts to human nature when it comes to fear is much more than an analogy: it's a scientific fact, and it has to do with the structure of the brain. Which is what we are going to talk about now.

THE NETWORK OF FEAR IN YOUR HEAD

Say what you like about brain damage, but a good whack to the head – in the right place – can do wonders for your bank balance. You see, normal people who feel fear worry about things. They worry, for example, about putting all their money into a risky investment and ending up with nothing. But people with damage to a certain area of their brains have little or no fear, and so they just go right ahead and do it, and to hell with the consequences. And sometimes it pays off.

In a study published in 2005 in the journal *Psychological Science*,[43] a team of researchers from Carnegie Mellon University, the Stanford Graduate School of Business and the University of Iowa got a range of people to play an investment game in which they were given money which they could either keep, or else gamble for the chance of making more money. Fifteen of the people in the experiment had damage to their brains that affected their ability to experience fear and other emotions, and these people all showed themselves to be far more willing to take risks that yielded high payoffs than the people without the brain damage. More than this, when they lost money they weren't particularly bothered. The result was that at the end of the game, they ended up 13 per cent better off, on average, than the other group. So there's your tip for financial success: if you want to get ahead, get your head knocked about a bit. You might experience a few downsides when you lose your emotions and your sense of fear: you may, for example, find yourself talking like Mr Spock from *Star Trek*, which other people might find irritating. Or you may find yourself behaving in a way which is cold, calculating and lacking in not only fear but shame and remorse besides – all classic signs of your being a psychopath – which other people might find very worrying indeed. So I wouldn't recommend it, on balance.

Let's have a look at this in a little more detail.

There is an answer, you see, to the question of fear, and why it feels the way it does, and why we find ourselves torn, at moments of crisis, between conflicting urges. There's even an answer to why it seems to make sense to talk of professors and dogs. This answer is to be found in the structure of your brain. In particular, it is to be found in a collection of 'organs' and connections within it, all centred around a region called the *amygdala* (four syllables, *a-mig-da-la*), which are collectively known as the *fear network*.[44] It's a network that has, to simplify slightly, a part that thinks and a part that deals in emotions and the memory of past emotions.

First the 'thinking' part of it. Your brain looks, from the outside, very much like a cauliflower. The thing that gives it this cauliflower-like appearance is the rippled outer layer, which is called the cortex, a word that comes originally from Latin, where it means 'bark' (as in tree rather than dog). It's in this outer layer that most of our conscious thinking takes place; and, in your case, it's what's weighing up these words you're reading right now.

Different areas of the cortex have different roles and functions, but the area that concerns us most, from the point of view of the fear network, is situated just forward from the crown of your head. This is known as the prefrontal cortex, and is where your conscious thoughts and goals are translated into actions. It's where what you think of as your personality gets translated into the way that you dress and speak and behave. It's where you decide, and act on, what is and isn't correct social behaviour: it stops you scratching your backside in public, among other things. So think of it as the central headquarters of the conscious control of behaviour.

Now for the feeling part of the fear network, the

amygdala. The amygdala is a little almond-shaped 'organ' – the name is Latin for almond – and it lives deep inside the core of your brain. It is much older in its evolutionary origin than the cortex and altogether different in function. Where the cortex deals in thoughts, the amygdala deals in emotions and the memory of emotions. Where the cortex deals in logic and deduction and right and wrong, the amygdala deals in the shifting currents of feeling. And in particular, the amygdala is right at the very centre of almost all of the brain events associated with the feeling of fear.

It's worth taking a brief detour here, on the subject of mice. Not metaphorical or figurative mice, though, because this is not a metaphorical or figurative chapter. We're talking about real mice. And not just any common or garden mice, but special mice, mutant mice, mice genetically engineered in a laboratory by a real professor by the name of Vadim Y. Bolshakov.[45] What Bolshakov did was to knock out a single gene from mouse embryos, which meant that the resulting mice were unable to produce a protein called stathmin. The function of stathmin in the brain is to help nerve cells make connections within the amygdala. And because amygdala cells in the mutant mice weren't able to form connections, these mice didn't develop fears in the same way that normal mice did, to the extent that, faced with a large and hungry cat, they were perfectly happy to wander up and have a good sniff round rather than scuttling for cover. If these mice could have played financial investment games, for cheese, say, it is likely that they would have ended considerably better off than normal mice. Either that, or bankrupt. Or, in the outside world, swiftly lining the inside of a cat's stomach.

So the amygdala is central to the feeling of fear, and an inactive or underactive amygdala will leave you without fear, for good or ill. An overactive amygdala, on the other hand, will make you a fearful, gibbering wreck. When it does work properly, though, and when it does create fear as it should, it does so in conjunction with a third brain structure, the *hippocampus*, which is where memories are stored.

The amygdala sits right next to the hippocampus in the brain, and from the hippocampus it collects memories of powerful emotions you have either experienced yourself, or else witnessed in the expressions and behaviours of other people. When the amygdala experiences something new, it quickly matches it up with these stored memories, and causes you to feel the appropriate emotion.

So that's the fear network. It's the prefrontal cortex, on the one hand, doing the thinking and playing the 'professor' role; and the amygdala, on the other, using memories from the hippocampus, doing the feeling and playing the 'dog' role. And with it being made up the way it is, of separate thinking and feeling parts, you can see how, in certain circumstances, you can get a bit of internal conflict in the system. Such as when you're standing with an arrow at your throat, for example, and the cortex has listened to the explanation and worked out that it's safe to walk forward, while the amygdala has conjured up visions of Custer's last stand and the dread and pain involved in piercing injuries, and says, in effect, 'over my dead body!'

So how is the conflict between the parts reconciled? Which wins? And how, and why?

A couple more facts about the fear network.

The first thing to say is that the brain is 'wired' so that your experiences, transmitted as impulses down your nerves, go straight to the amygdala, which checks them against the emotional memories stored in the hippo-campus and, if it deems it necessary, activates the *startle reaction*, preparing your body to run or to fight. Only then, when the amygdala's done its thing, are the stimuli passed up a series of nerves to your cortex, which takes a moment to analyse them to see whether the apparent threat is real or not, and then passes a recommendation back down a secondary circuit to the amygdala. So your emotionally driven amygdala gets the information before the rationally driven cortex, and gets its reaction in first.

The second thing to say is that the pathway up from your amygdala to your cortex is both thicker and faster than the secondary pathway in the opposite direction. So in any conflict between the two, your amygdala has the advantage.[46]

What all this means is that when it comes to fear and danger, we are always in two minds about the nature of the risks we face and what to do about them, even if we aren't always aware of it at the time. We deal with things in two separate ways – an emotional way and a rational way, or a 'professor' way and a 'dog' way – but of the two, emotion takes priority. Emotion has a far greater power and influence over thinking than thinking ever has over emotion. Once an emotion has been turned on, it is very, very hard for the thinking mind to turn it off again. 'At this point in our evolutionary history,' says the neuroscientist Joseph LeDoux, 'while conscious control over emotions is weak, emotions can flood consciousness.'[47] As Charles Darwin discovered, when he tried to prove the power of reason over emotion at the local zoo:

> I put my face close to the thick glass-plate in front
> of a puff-adder in the Zoological Gardens, with the

firm determination of not starting back if the snake struck at me; but, as soon as the blow was struck, my resolution went for nothing, and I jumped a yard or two backwards with astonishing rapidity. My will and reason were powerless . . .'[48]

You might be tempted to wonder why all this is the case, though.

You might be tempted to wonder why we have two different ways of dealing with danger, and why they fight with each other, and what the point of it is, and why it has to be that way rather than some other way.

If you've ever found yourself at the mercy of your emotions, and it's sapped your courage and stopped you from doing what you knew to be the right and good thing to do, you might have thought about this. If you've ever made a resolution to eat healthier food, or to give up smoking, or to take more exercise, for the good of your health and in the certain knowledge that you are right so to do, and then found yourself, five minutes later, caving in in the face of uncontrollable emotional cravings, you will certainly have thought about it. Why can't we just do what we know in our heads to be right? Why does emotion have to stick its oar in? How come we've evolved to be the way we are?

We would have evolved that way, with thinking being in sole command of all of the important decisions affecting our safety, if thinking alone were capable of getting us to the right answer better than thinking and emotion together.

If thinking were such a good thing, people who did more of it, and less emoting, would, over the generations, have been more likely to survive the dangers of the past, and, by now, the power of the emotions would be a lot weaker. But they weren't, and it isn't. The people who were best at surviving the dangers of the past were the ones who lived long enough to pass their genes on to us. Which is to say, they were pretty much the same as we are.

There's a problem with thinking, you see. Wonderful as it is, it has limitations, and these limitations can be very dangerous indeed, without something else to keep our thoughts in check.

The good thing about thinking – and also the bad thing about thinking – is that it's clever. Which is to say it's abstract and theoretical and it lives inside your head. It can encompass all sorts of wonderful possibilities beyond what we can physically experience here and now. Because of thinking, we've got computers and railway trains, televisions and motor cars. Because of thinking, we understand the world in a way that we never could through experience alone: we understand all about black holes and sub-atomic particles, and all of those sorts of things.

But thinking has also come up with some real stinkers – the sorts of things that someone who didn't think would never be stupid enough to believe in. There are people who believe that cancer can be cured by the laying-on of hands and the muttering of words. There are people who believe that the moon landings were faked; people who believe that Princess Diana was murdered by MI5 agents using strobe lights and, for some reason, a small, white Fiat Uno; people who believe that the planes that crashed into the Twin Towers were not planes at all, but holograms of planes to disguise the Secret Service missiles or explosive charges that 'really' did it; and there are people who believe that the world is secretly ruled by shape-shifting seven-foot-tall lizards, whose human forms include Bill and Hillary Clinton, George W. Bush and members of the British royal family.

The thing about thinking, you see, is that it depends on a chain of logic. If you get one weak link somewhere along the way, one untested assumption that doesn't stack up against reality, then everything else that follows can cause you to drift further and further from the way things really are; and if you entrust your health, your safety or your life to it, then you could come badly unstuck.

And the argument of this book, as a matter of fact, is incontrovertible proof of that, whether you agree with it or not. Especially, in fact, if you don't agree with it. Because I got to where we've ended up by thinking; and if you think I've ended up in the wrong place, or am drawing wrong conclusions, that just goes to show how thinking can lead you in the wrong direction. So if I'm right, I'm right. And if I'm wrong, that just goes to show that I'm right.

A distant relative of mine had her leg off because she refused a blood transfusion, on account of being a Jehovah's Witness. And then she died.

It's not just people who aren't very good at thinking who get themselves into ridiculous situations by paying too much attention to what's in their heads and not enough to what's under their noses. Sometimes it seems that the greater your capacity for abstract thinking, the greater your capacity for going off down blind alleys and, sometimes, coming a cropper because of it. There have been some extraordinarily clever people over the years who have managed to persuade themselves of some spectacularly stupid things after becoming caught up in their own cleverness.

There are academic philosophers who claim that the laws of physics and mathematics are arbitrary and made up by 'society', and that there is no such thing as absolute truth. (Yeah, right, mate – so you go and jump off of that cliff, then, and we'll see whether you end up absolutely dead or not, shall we?)

Then there was Sir Isaac Newton – a contender for the title of the Greatest Thinker of All Time, if ever there was one – who managed somehow to persuade himself of some ideas about alchemy and magic that were, quite frankly, stark raving bonkers. In the course of his 'experiments' to turn lead into gold, he ended up inhaling so much mercury vapour that it killed him. So that's where thinking can lead you if you pay too much attention to it, and not enough attention to your emotions.

And then, on the other side, there's what would happen to you if you didn't think at all, and just went wherever your emotions pulled you. It wouldn't be a pretty sight.

So that's why you have evolved with two separate and different ways of dealing with danger, and why they sometimes fight with each other. Each keeps the wilder excesses of the other in check, and together they achieve a sort of compromise, which, though not perfect every time, has worked a lot better for a lot longer than either of the alternatives.

As for the precise balance of power between the two, with emotion having the upper hand (most of the time) and the final say (most of the time) in any conflict, that is the balance that has worked best, over many hundreds of thousands of years, in the kind of world in which we evolved.

To understand why this should be the case, imagine yourself as a primitive ape-man in the distant past, or a modern-day chimpanzee in a forest in Africa, living under constant threat from predators – leopards, say, with fast reflexes and lots of sharp teeth, or snakes with poison fangs, or even violent rivals of your own species, out to take your territory from you. In those sorts of circumstances, it pays to worry most about visible dangers that cause sudden, violent and nasty death, and it pays to act first and analyse later. It pays, moreover, for your visceral instinct to fight for your life, or to run for your life, to be able to override any tendency to ponder on the deeper meaning of your situation.

It may not have escaped your notice, though, that nowadays most of us no longer live in the kind of world in which we evolved, in terms of being out in the open on the savannahs of East Africa, and that the kind of world in which we now live has changed, in quite a few important respects, from the way it used to be when we were all called Ugg or Ogg or things like that, and hunted sabre-tooth mammoths with flint-tipped arrows.

The fact that we no longer live in that kind of world, as it happens, is causing us rather a lot of problems nowadays in the way that we react to fear and danger, and the things we do, and it's leading us into error and foolishness. It's not our fault, as such: we don't do it on purpose, or set out to be stupid just to annoy everyone – it's just that, in a high-tech, fast-moving world, we've still got caveman brains. And this means that nowadays we worry too much about things that aren't really a threat to us, and not enough about certain things that are.

WHY WE WORRY TOO MUCH

How often do you see a leopard out to get you, eh? Or a snake? Not very often, I'd reckon. But if you were one of the chimps in the jungle we were talking about just now, you'd probably come across them a bit more often. And to the extent that you saw them, or the results of a leopard or snake attack on a member of your pack, or the emotions of other members of your pack upon seeing a leopard or a snake, that would determine the extent to which your brain would judge the seriousness of the risk, and the extent that you would develop a fear of them. Makes sense, doesn't it?

At the heart of this rather commonsensical process is your amygdala, acting on the frequency and severity of emotional responses to leopards and snakes you experience, or witness, and which are stored as memories in your hippocampus. Lots of experiences of emotional upheaval, or very severe and intense experiences of emotional upheaval, means lots of warning memories in your hippocampus, or very severe and intense war markers in your hippocampus, which means lots of fear generated in your amygdala.

It's an animal thing. It works simply and powerfully, and exactly as it should, without the need for rational or abstract thought to complicate things.

But it only works simply and powerfully and exactly as it should when the experiences you have correspond to the way the world actually is. Which, in the wild, it does. Because in the wild, you experience emotions to do with leopards to roughly the extent that leopards actually impinge on the world in which you live.

But here's the catch: the number and kind of dangers and emotional upheavals that we experience today no longer correspond to the way the world we live in actually is. This is because we experience the world, more and more, through the media – which is to say, through television, through the Internet and through newspapers.

If you experience the world through the television, through the Internet and through newspapers, you will see a very different world from the one that you actually live in, and you will experience, every day, all sorts of emotions brought about by dangers that you are never likely come across in your daily life, even if you should live to be a hundred years old or more.

You will see a whole range of disasters, crimes and catastrophes that you could go a whole lifetime without ever getting caught up in yourself. There will be senseless murders, there will be child abductions, there will be violent crime, there will be horrifying diseases, and – to get back to the fear of flying – there will be plane crashes. And the more television you watch, the more Internet pages you look at and the more newspapers you read, the more often and the more intensely your emotions will be affected. And your amygdala sitting there inside you and experiencing all of these dangers and all of this emotional upheaval, and not being big on statistics or abstract thought, will begin to assume that this is the way the world is.

The more immediate and realistic the media, the more you can put names and faces to the people involved, and the more you feel you 'know' the victims, then the worse it gets, and the more you feel a palpable threat to your own safety and that of your family. This is something most of us sense instinctively.

You'll have felt the distinction yourself if you've ever been brought up short by a shocking-sounding announce-ment on the radio, something like 'HUNDREDS KILLED IN HORRIFIC TRAIN CRASH . . . ' and thought, 'Oh my God!' only for the announcer to finish his sentence with

'. . . IN CHINA' (or some other country you've never been to, don't much care about and don't know anyone who lives in); and you've breathed a sigh of relief – guiltily or otherwise – and carried on with whatever it was you were doing. Alternatively you may have come across worthy souls like Dickens's Mrs. Jellyby, who really *do* care about all sorts of people they've never met, and who care so much about them that they seem to have little concern left for their own families or neighbours.

It seems that there are only so many individual people we can fit into our sphere of concern. This is something that Josef Stalin (who knew a thing or two about death and disaster) put his finger on when he talked about one death being a tragedy and a million deaths being a statistic. There's actually a good scientific reason for this. You see, there are limits to the number of people you can fit into your head, and limits to the number of people you can know enough to care about personally, or to feel a sense of relationship with or connection to. It's a physical thing, this capacity, and it's constrained by the size of the outer layer or cortex of your brain, the thinking part that we talked about earlier.

Studies on antelopes, monkeys and apes and a wide range of other mammal species suggest that there's a clear and straightforward relationship: the bigger the cortex, the greater the number of individuals who can form a meaningful part of your group or the structures of recognition and concern you hold inside your head. Beyond the right size for your species, groups begin to fall apart and split into smaller units.

The first study to propose the idea of an 'ideal number' was one carried out in the early 1990s by the anthropologist Robin Dunbar, of London's University College.[49] By comparing the average sizes of a range of different kinds of ape and monkey groups with the volume of their cortexes, and by extrapolating that to the volume of the human cortex, he came up with a theoretical relationship that puts our 'natural' group size at somewhere around 150 (147.8 was his figure, now known as 'Dunbar's number'). In practice, the number is rarely quite so precise (even without the 0.8) and Dunbar proposed a broader set of bounds, depending on circumstances, at between 100 and 230 individuals – which is roughly the range of group sizes in which modern-day hunter-gatherer bands live.

Anyway, to bring this all back to the point about the media: the more successful it is in broadcasting images and creating stories which bring news events to life and which tug at your heartstrings, the more you admit the victims, in your mind, into your personal 150 – into the circle of people whose names and faces you recognize and who mean something to you. And if this happens regularly, it begins to feel as if known members of your personal band are dropping like flies, and suffering the most awful things on an almost-daily basis. Which makes you start to think about your own safety – even if, rationally speaking, the actual odds of some of these things happening to you are many millions to one. Emotionally, your brain doesn't do advanced statistics, and it doesn't work in millions: it feels, and works, on an individual level, up to 150. Beyond that and – like Stalin – you're talking statistics.

So you shouldn't be at all surprised, living in a modern society with more and more access to more and more media, bringing more and more terrible events and horribly unfortunate people directly and vividly into your life and your experience, to find yourself, and the people around you, becoming steadily more fearful about 'dangers' that earlier generations wouldn't have given a second thought to and which, if you take the trouble to analyse them properly, are actually very, very unlikely to happen to you or to anyone you know.

After 'experiencing' plane crashes in the news, and seeing the looks on the faces of the grieving relatives, you might get the shakes at the thought of getting on a plane, for fear of crashing. After seeing lines of policemen pacing through scrubland searching for a missing child, and after seeing the tearful pleas of the parents to the abductor who, you just know, has already killed the terrified child horribly, you might well stop letting your children go out to play on their own, for fear that the same will happen to them. You might stop trusting strangers, for fear of crime. And on top of all this, you might start to develop an overwhelming feeling that the world is becoming a far more dangerous and worrying place than it used to be when you were young.

We're not rational in our fears, and we're not statistically correct in them, either. That's the nature of fear. Fear is a very good and very effective emotional system designed by evolution for the real world as it existed throughout most of human history. But unfortunately for us, that isn't the world we live in now. As a consequence our system of fear has been overloaded and overdosed with distorted information. It tries to do the best it can, but it is saddled with an unreal picture of the terrors and disasters that surround it.

And that's why we worry too much.

But if you don't realize that, if you think that things really are getting more dangerous, then you might start thinking that what we really need is more safety laws and restrictions, more guidelines and directives, to sort these worrying dangers out, and to make things safe again. And that, you think, will make people feel safe and happy once more.

Except it won't. If anything, it will just make things worse.

You might worry too much about a particular danger, but if you believe that you have the ultimate responsibility for dealing with it, you at least have some power to take action and reduce your fear. If you can do that, you can – to some extent – put it out of your mind. Your brain can set up a strategy for dealing with the problem if it arises, and then get on with other things. Whereas if it's out of your hands, if there is no strategy you can adopt, if you feel wholly dependent on the vigilance and actions of others to keep you safe, then it becomes a very big worry indeed.

This is why, to take one example, some people get much more worked up about preservatives in their food than by the prospect of going on a family skiing holiday.[50] This is despite the fact that skiing is a thousand times more risky, from the point of view of serious incapacity or premature death, than preservatives; and that it is especially so for desk-bound people who do little or no regular exercise, and who ski no more than a week or two a year.

The fact that people are more worried by things outside their control means that passing more safety regulations and instituting more official precautions and procedures can often have precisely the opposite effect to that which is intended. They take the power and the responsibility away from individual people to deal with the dangers that face them. They make them depend on 'the authorities' for their safety, rather than on their own resources, and so they are diminished in their ability to act for themselves and less able to cope, and this has the effect of making them more fearful, rather than less so.

It is for these reasons that many people in the 'developed' world today exist in a state of rising paranoia and panic about the threats, both real and imagined, that face them and, especially, that face their children.

It is a world of predatory strangers, of tainted food, of suspect vaccinations, of looming pandemics. It is a world in which you can buy your children sweatshirts lined with stab-resistant Kevlar, and school blazers fitted with tracking devices. It is a world in which teachers are no longer allowed to apply a sticking-plaster to a child's cut, in case it should be thought 'inappropriate'. It is a world, in short, in which everyone and everything is out to get you.

And meanwhile, in all of the hysteria about all these

new fears we face, we somehow manage to overlook some very real dangers which don't always make it into the media. Like what happens, for example, to children who stay indoors all their lives and never go out to play, and who never have the freedom or the life-lessons that their own parents had.

WHY WE DON'T WORRY ENOUGH

Aeroplanes: remember what we said earlier about your chance of being involved in a plane crash? You'd have to take a flight a day for 26,000 years before being involved in a crash. Smoking: rather more risky than flying, in the sense that over half of all people who smoke regularly die because of it; and yet you get people who light up to help them overcome their fear of flying. What's going on there?

Again, it's a brain thing.

The 'animal' side of our brain, the bit that makes us afraid, the bit that makes our blood pump and our hands sweat and our heart leap in our chest, that part isn't big on abstract thought, as we know.

It distrusts words and concepts. It likes to go by what it sees and feels. And it likes to see and feel one thing followed by another, action followed by consequence, cause followed by effect – or cause followed by what appears, to all intents and purposes, to be effect.

A plane crashes into a building; people die. Across the world, fear of flying goes through the roof, and – as we've already seen – to calm people down airports have to bring in theatrical and intrusive security measures which often have little practical preventative effect on would-be terrorists. What these security measures are really doing is stroking people, saying, 'There, there, calm down: you don't have to worry. We've got it all in hand.'

A child has a combined measles, mumps and rubella vaccination. A short time later, that child shows the first signs of autism. And it happens not once, not twice, but thousands of times, all across the country. People get scared. The doctors do research, and they report back that it's all just coincidence – the age at which the MMR vaccination is given just so happens to be the age at which autism begins to show itself. But to the animal side of the brain those are just empty words: it has seen, with its own eyes, the suffering children, the distraught parents, and felt the pain of it; and whatever words the doctors have to say, it doesn't want to hear. So people stop having their children vaccinated. And a short while later doctors notice that measles is making a comeback.[51] This is a disease that used to kill twenty British children every year, until MMR came along and cut the death-toll to a total of one, in all the years since. But an emotion once turned on is hard to turn off using words and statistics. So medical science says there is no link between MMR and autism? This is because there is an Establishment 'cover-up'. So the government announces the return of measles? This is because they are exaggerating the figures, to draw attention away from the problems of MMR. And so on, and so forth.

The rains fail. Crops wither. The earth cracks. People and animals begin to die. A goat is sacrificed to the rain gods. The rains come. And the animal part of your brain sees action and consequence, cause and effect.

But there is a reverse side to all of this, which is what happens when people are faced with dangers that show no obvious pattern of cause and effect.

There are things in this world that may be invisible to the eye and impossible to taste, smell or touch, but which can kill you, gradually, over the course of years or decades. But because we do not experience the 'first this, then that' feeling of direct cause and effect, and because death can come about many, many years after your last exposure to whatever it was that kills you, we find it hard to see or feel the danger, and hard to rouse ourselves to the appropriate level of fear.

My wife tells me that at secondary school, as a teenager, she and her friends once scratched and sniffed the asbestos mats used in chemistry, in the hope of getting a couple of days off school, sick, through contracting asbestosis. Asbestosis kills you, horribly. It destroys your lungs and you end up choking to death slowly. The thing about asbestos dust is that it can sit there, biding its time, for forty years or more after you so much as even saw a piece of asbestos, before it finally shows itself. Would she have tried to get time off school through a more immediate and obvious cause of death, like jumping off the science-block roof? I very much doubt it. And yet the end results of both asbestosis and jumping are precisely the same: you die. But if you stand unsupported on the parapet of a tall building, and if you stand unprotected beside a sack of asbestos dust, the level of fear you will feel in each case will be of a wholly different order.

Asbestos is just one of a whole range of chemicals that destroy the body, but so slowly that you don't notice it. There are *carcinogens*, which cause cancer. There are *mutagens*, which cause malformations in your genetic material. There are *teratogens*, which can cause malformations in a developing foetus. And the world we live in today may be swarming with them: we just don't know. There are so many new materials all around us, and we don't yet know what the full long-term effects of living with them are. So your MDF cupboards or the paint on your walls may be sitting there, giving off invisible vapours that may one day put you in a wooden box, just as surely as unprotected exposure to asbestos dust did to an earlier generation.

Some of these substances may be in our environment or in our food at too low a level to pose any real danger to us, on their own – but when they combine they can be deadly, either by magnifying each other's effects, as cigarette smoke and asbestos dust do when they meet, or else by one acting as a catalyst to unleash the carcinogenic effects of another.[52]

There's danger there: it's just that it's not the sort of danger that our emotions find it easy to see obvious cause and effect in, and, consequently, we don't get too worked up about it.

Which brings us back to smoking. On the one hand, we absolutely know that it's bad for us. We've always known it's bad for us. In 1604, King James the First wrote scornfully of 'a custome loathsome to the eye, hatefull to the nose, harmefull to the braine [and] dangerous to the lungs'.[53] But on the other hand, there's a huge separation between cause and effect, such that you never see someone take one puff of a cigarette and then keel over immediately, or in a day or two, or even in a year or two. And though many smokers do eventually die of it, not all of them do; and the ones who are left are the ones we see still carrying on like normal. So it's always possible to point to the sprightly ninety-year-old, who's been smoking like a chimney since the age of five, and never felt better for it.

So what smokers see, and what they feel, when they light up, is relaxation, sociability and, perhaps, an air of slightly disreputable sophistication. It doesn't root you to the spot in fear. And although the thinking mind may come up with all sorts of intellectual arguments and facts against it, for many people these are contradicted by the evidence of their own senses. As a result, people don't tend to develop a raw, physical terror of cigarettes. The most you get is disapproval, which isn't the same thing at all.

That's one side of the way we are: when it comes to picking the things we should be afraid of, and the things we shouldn't, we often get it wrong.

There's another side, too: there are some things that we choose to do precisely because they make us frightened, and because of the things we get from them, on top of the fear itself. And that's what we're going to talk about now.

PART FOUR

THE JOY OF FEAR

THE RISK TAKERS

John Mytton – later to be known as 'Mad Jack' Mytton, for reasons that will soon become apparent – was born in Shropshire on 30 September 1796.[54] He was orphaned shortly afterwards, and left in possession of his father's country estate, Halston Hall, and a vast fortune, which, as soon as he was able to, he set about spending in pursuit of the one thing he cared about – excitement.

He found it hard to settle to anything he regarded as dull. Expelled from Westminster School in his first year for fighting, he then moved on to Harrow, where he lasted just three days. Then, when no other school would take him, he went through a string of short-lived private tutors, many of whom left quickly after failing to see the funny side of 'practical jokes' like finding a horse in their bedroom. Next, he went up to Cambridge, taking 2,000 bottles of port with him, but soon became bored and left without graduating. He tried and abandoned a Grand Tour of Europe, a spell in the army and even a career in

Parliament. He'd bought his way into Westminster by giving a ten-pound note to everyone who voted for him, but after watching just half an hour of one Westminster debate he left, never to return.

Instead, he filled his time drinking and gambling and hunting, pursuing each with a recklessness that astounded those who saw him. On the hunting field, wearing one of his 700 pairs of hand-made riding boots, he would charge his horse at impossible jumps, to see what happened. What happened, generally, was that he came off and broke a rib or two. Then he would pick himself up, dust himself off and carry on with the hunt, 'unmurmuring' in the words of one contemporary report, 'when every jar was an agony'. He also loved to race his carriages down narrow country lanes, tearing round bends and across crossroads without looking, and driving straight at rabbit holes and other obstacles, to see if he would crash. He frequently did. Once, he drove his carriage at a toll gate to see if the horse could jump it. It couldn't. On another occasion he was driving a gig in his usual manner when his terrified companion made the mistake of admitting that he had never been in a road accident before. 'What!' exclaimed Mytton. 'What a damn slow fellow you must have been all your life!' And with that, he headed off the road at full speed and up a bank, overturning the gig and tipping them both out.

Nor were the evenings any safer than the daytimes for Mytton's companions. One evening he invited the local parson and doctor to dinner, but jumped out at them on their journey disguised as a highwayman, crying 'Stand and deliver!' and firing pistols over their heads, causing them to flee for their lives. At another dinner party he turned up dressed in full hunting kit, mounted on the back of a bear. As his friends started from the table in panic and some climbed out of the windows, Mytton called out, 'Tally ho!' and dug his spurs into the bear, which promptly turned its head and sank its teeth into his calf.

Even with an annual income worth three-quarters of a million pounds by today's standards, his profligacy was immense, and he was eventually forced to flee to France to escape his creditors. While he was there, and finding himself with a bout of the hiccups, he decided to try a novel way to cure himself. Taking a lighted candle, he applied the flame to the tail of his starched cotton shirt and was instantly engulfed in flames. As his servant beat out the fire, leaving him covered in raw burns 'the same colour as a newly singed bacon hog', he cried out, 'Well, the hiccup is gone, by God!'

This kind of existence takes its toll. It tends not to be a sensible strategy for a long and contented life. If it were, he might have ended up with a different nickname, 'Sensible Jack', perhaps, or 'Normal Jack'; or maybe, like many of us, he wouldn't have been thought out of the ordinary enough to warrant a nickname at all. As it was, 'Mad Jack' returned to England, where he was locked up in a debtors' prison in Southwark before dying at the age of thirty-eight. By that time he was, in the words of a contemporary account, 'a round-shouldered, tottering old-young man bloated by drink, worn out by too much foolishness, too much wretchedness and too much brandy'.

We're not all the same, as far as taking risks is concerned.

Some people actively seek out the sensations and rewards to be gained from overcoming danger while others prefer the steady benefits of a safe and quiet life.

Professor Marvin Zuckerman of the University of Delaware has been studying this phenomenon since the 1960s. In 1971 he produced his highly influential theory of *Sensation Seeking*, which holds that your propensity to take risks in the pursuit of pleasure and novelty is, to a large extent, a fixed part of your personality. Since then, he has explored the mechanisms by which this personality characteristic comes about. His conclusion, based on twin-comparison studies and summarized in *Psychology Today* in November 2000,[55] was that the main difference between sensation seekers, who take more risks, and other people, who take fewer risks, is genetic: it's a tendency you inherit, to a very large degree, from your parents.

To put it in some sort of perspective: when scientists talk about something in your personality having a high degree of heritability – which is to say it is greatly influenced by the genes passed on to you by your parents – they usually mean that about 30 to 50 per cent of the reason you're like this is down to your genes.

With this particular trait – the willingness to take risks – studies quoted by Zuckerman estimate about 60 per cent being attributable to your genes, which is very high indeed, and more important than any other factor. As a result, bank managers tend to beget little bank managers, and stunt men and stunt women tend to beget stunt babies and stunt toddlers.

The reason we aren't all equally brave, and why all the very cautious people, or all the very foolhardy people, haven't died out, is that there is no 'correct' approach to danger – just an acceptable range of approaches that sort of work – and in any individual situation it's down to the luck of the draw whether your approach works best.

In some situations brave people succeed, and in other situations cautious people do better.

Bravery is a high-risk strategy. It can bring great rewards, but it can bring equally grave dangers. Some of the biggest risk takers can end up being spectacularly successful, if conditions are right. Genghis Khan, for example, risked death on more occasions than you could shake a stick at, but he survived them all and lived to pass on his genes through so many women, to so many children, that today it is estimated that there are 16 million living men in the world who share his Y-chromosome – and, it might be assumed, a similar number of women also directly descended from him. To put it another way, Ghengis, with his risk-taking genes, has 800,000 times more surviving descendants than the average man of his time.[56]

However, Genghis Khan could easily have ended up like Alexander the Great. Alexander also lived a brave and dangerous life, but as a consequence he coughed it a little short of his thirty-third birthday, passing his risk-taking genes on to just one son, who also died young.

As well as risk-taking genes, people like Genghis Khan and Alexander the Great tend to have something else in common: testosterone. In general, the more you have of it to go with your risk-taking genes, the more risks you take. Men have more of it than women, and take more risks at all ages. Younger men have more than older men, which means that men are twice as likely to take risks in their late teens than they are by the time they reach their fifties – assuming they survive the risks they took in their teens, that is. And some men, of whatever age, have more testosterone than others; and these men are the ones, all other things being equal, who take the most risks of all.[57]

THE JOY OF FEAR

There are two sides to getting frightened. There's fear itself, and what it feels like when you're afraid – which generally, isn't very nice at all – and then there's what happens when you overcome your fear, and when you survive the danger that faced you, or when you triumph over it.

This can feel very nice indeed. It's a feeling of competence, of mastery, of success in the face of adversity, a feeling of being wholly and physically alive, right here and right now. For some people, in fact – and we'll talk about what kinds of people they are in just a moment, and what they have about them that makes them the way they are – it can feel like the very best thing in the world.

The reason it can feel so good to triumph over a threat is because of what goes on in your brain when that happens. First thing is your amygdala goes on full alert, and adrenalin rushes around your body, increasing your heart rate and your breathing, widening your eyes, waking up your muscles, all to get you ready to fight or to run. In the scientific journals, by the way, adrenalin goes by the name of epinephrine, for some reason or other.

So anyway, this adrenalin or epinephrine, it gets you going, gets you ready for action. Then you're ready to do whatever it is that you need to do in order to survive.

And then, when you've done it, and when you've overcome whatever it was that was threatening you, your brain releases a second chemical called *dopamine* (just dopamine at the moment – they haven't changed the name to anything else yet, as far as I'm aware), and that makes you feel good. In fact, a big dose of it, after a big scare, makes you feel more than good: it makes you feel euphoric. And so it should. What's happening is that you are being rewarded for surviving, rewarded for doing whatever it was that you did to save your life. Your brain is saying, 'Well done! Keep it up, old chap! And if you do, there's more where that came from.'

And it's interesting to note here that some people, because of their genetic make-up, have a stronger reaction to the dopamine reward than others – and this is one of the things that goes towards making them likely risk takers. Two separate studies in Israel and in the USA have both implicated a gene called the dopamine receptor-4 gene. There are two versions of it that you could possibly have: a long version and a short one. Risk takers tend to have the long version while cautious people tend to have the short version.[58]

'There is nothing,' as Sir Winston Churchill put it, 'so exhilarating in life as to be shot at without effect.'

But, he might have added, it's especially exhilarating if you happen to have a long dopamine receptor gene.

Surviving danger is so important that it is not surprising that people get pleasure from it. All living creatures do – even insects, which have a substance called *octopamine* (it was first discovered in the saliva of octopuses. Or is it octopi?) which fills the role of dopamine in humans.[59] You can imagine a little fly, frantically trying to struggle its way free of a spider's web as the spider is bearing down on it, breaking away just in time and then feeling a huge wave of pleasure and relief.

But there's a balance to be struck in these things. It's a balance between the pleasure you get from surviving and the terror you feel from being in dangerous situations in the first place. Any fly that launched itself repeatedly into spiders' webs for the 'buzz' it got from breaking free at the last minute wouldn't be long for this world; and any soldier who strolled casually up and down in front of enemy snipers in order to enjoy being 'shot at without effect' would soon find himself being shot at with very serious effect indeed.

But on the other hand, listening only to fear and never going anywhere or taking any risks isn't such a good idea either, from the point of surviving for long enough to pass your genes on to the next generation. If you were a fly, you would find that the food you need to keep you alive is all out there where the spiders lurk; and if you were a soldier, you would find that hiding from the enemy and never firing a shot in anger will protect you only until the enemy overruns your position and comes to seek you out.

What you find is that each species will arrive at a general balance between being brave and being timid, with slight variations from individual to individual. We're actually quite a risk-taking species, as species go: and because of that we've managed, in the space of little more than 100,000 years, to go from being a bunch of monkeys (hominids, if you want to be strictly correct about this) somewhere in Africa to more or less total world domination. Not to mention flying to the moon. A big part of what started that change was the willing-ness of groups of men to give up the constant foraging for berries and roots and start taking the risks involved in hunting dangerous big game. But there have been a lot of cock-ups along the way, and a lot of deaths through foolhardy experiments and adventures gone wrong. As people like Scott of the Antarctic would no doubt be able to tell you, if it weren't for the fact that they are well and truly dead.

PLAYING WITH DANGER

As well as some people having genes that make them more – or less – likely to take risks than others; and as well as all of us having genes that make us, as a species, more likely to enjoy trying new and untested things than most other species, human beings also have one or two genes that make us cleverer, on the whole, than most other species.

Put all this together and what you find is that people, over the ages, have developed ways of getting more of the pleasure that comes from surviving risk, with less of the actual risk itself.

We do this by playing at danger.

Playing at danger involves games or sports which allow us to fool ourselves into believing that we really are facing and overcoming mortal peril, when in fact we are doing nothing of the kind – or, at least, when we are doing a lot less of the kind than it appears.

To be precise about this, when I say 'we' fool 'ourselves',

it's probably more accurate to say that the thinking mind is the thing doing the fooling, and the emotional, animal side of us, the amygdala, is the thing that's being fooled into believing it's in danger.

As for why you would want to do that, it's because of the pleasure to be had when the hormones kick in – the thrill and the euphoria, and the feeling of being so intensely alive. And also, whether we're aware of the fact or not, because it keeps the body and mind 'match-fit' and prepared and practised for when, or if, we have to face real dangers in life. And that makes a lot of sense, when it comes to surviving in the wild.

There's a sort of a sliding scale of dangerous play in which what you get out of it, in terms of the thrill and satisfaction, depends on what you put into it, and how convincing a show of danger you can make yourself experience – which, to some extent, depends on the degree of real physical risk involved. Also it depends on the amount of mental and physical skill and effort you need to use to overcome it: something that is very physically and mentally demanding tends, on the whole, to give a lot more pleasure and satisfaction than something that isn't. But then again, things that are more dangerous and demanding also carry with them a greater possibility of ending up in casualty, or dead, so there's a balance to be struck.

Probably the least convincing 'dangerous play' of all is watching a horror film. That's not to say a horror film won't scare you, or make your heart thump in your chest, or make you scream and dive on top of your boyfriend or girlfriend in terror at the bit at the end where you think it's all over and it's all nice soothing music and then suddenly the crazed hillbilly psycho you thought had been killed shoots up out of the lake with his bloodstained axe in his hand. But unlike TV news reports of the latest disease or terrorist threat, you know right from the start that it's only make-believe. More than this, you have eyes in your head, and these eyes can see, beyond the fictional world on the screen, the safe, comfortable room in which you and your companions are seated; and you will have all sorts of memories of television-watching and cinema-going stored in your brain that will tell you that however frightening a film may be, it's only a film and there has never, ever been a single reported case of a crazed hillbilly psycho – or indeed any other character from a film – suddenly breaking through the screen and out into the real world. Nor are there any consequences to your actions: whether you lounge back in your seat or stand up and yell out to the characters to watch out for what's waiting for them in the old barn with the flapping door, exactly the same thing will happen. In the film, that is: in the cinema, someone may tell you to sit down and shut up.

So on one level, you're there, but on another level something I'll call the corner-of-the-eye effect is telling you it's not really happening. Which means that although you will really get scared, you won't get anywhere near as scared as you would be if you really were being stalked by a genuine homicidal inbred hick in patched dungarees.

Next up is the video game. Again, it's 'only' make-believe, and it's only a projection on a screen, but this time you are in the world of the game – or mentally you are, at least. In a game, what you do, or fail to do, will have serious consequences for the characters. Depending on your actions, your character will either survive and prosper or else die in horrible ways. You, however, won't. Not unless you get so worked up that you have a heart attack. Which, though possible, is unlikely.

Game playing really does get the adrenalin going, though, and can hold the attention for hours on end. An intense session will make you feel highly strung and shaky afterwards – not least because in the real world that amount of fear and stimulation, for that length of time, would have had you doing some serious running or fighting, which would have burnt off a lot of the energy that you were worked up to, and would have left you feeling triumphantly calm at the end of it. As opposed to jittery, say, and bouncing off the walls, and unable to sleep. Again, though, there's this corner-of-the-eye effect thing to it as well. Even when you're most involved, even when you're fighting the fiercest dragon or scaling the impossible wall, or taking the last bend on the racetrack at unbelievable speed in the game, part of you can still see, and is still aware of, the fact that you're actually in your mate's bedroom, and part of you can hear his mum when she calls up asking if you boys want a cup of tea or anything, and mind you don't play for too long because you've got homework to do.

Then there are 'games' that involve real rather than imagined action, and real speeds and real opponents, and real-life dangers – or, at least, real things that give every impression to your amygdala of being dangerous, even if your thinking mind knows better. They do this by bringing in the appearance of real physical danger, and by eliminating as far as possible the reassurance of the corner-of-the-eye effect.

Perhaps the safest of the real-life scary games is the rollercoaster. Now, rollercoasters really are very safe. It's just that they don't look it or feel it. You may remember from earlier on in the book that only one in every 834 million rides goes wrong and kills someone, compared with one in every 43 million passenger rail journeys. Which is to say rollercoasters are nearly twenty times safer than trains, and both are a hell of a lot safer than most of the things that you've probably done today. Particularly if you've been in a car. Or a canoe, even. But the point is, though, that they don't seem at all safe when you're on them. You get in this rickety-looking little cart and you get winched up a huge great scaffold, and there seems to be nothing on either side of you to stop the cart falling off – no handrails or safety barriers or anything. And up and up you go, and you stop looking down because it churns your stomach up so much, and you curse yourself for having let yourself be persuaded to come on, and swear that if you ever make it out alive you will never, ever go near anything like this, ever again. And then you're at the top, and you can see, falling away ahead of you, a sheer drop the height of a skyscraper, and you cannot believe, just cannot compute, that any second now you are about to go over the edge, and that . . . and with a sickening lurch you're dropping, down and down and down, faster than you could ever imagine, down to the ground where surely you will be smashed into . . . but just at the last moment, just at the very last split-second you've swerved, pulled out of the dive, and you're alive, and no longer screaming but laughing, and you're on the way up again. And so it goes on.

With rollercoasters you begin to get a real separation between a thinking mind that absolutely knows that no harm will come to you and an amygdala that is fairly comprehensively convinced that you're about to die, and as a result your emotions, and your hormones, are all over the place. Which can be fun.

Whether it's a truly satisfying experience, though, is another question. There are people who would argue that it is: there are people who get so much of a buzz from it that they save up all their money and their holiday entitlement to travel the world just in order to ride the latest, biggest scariest ride.

Two things, though.

One is that although there is little or no corner-of-the-eye reassurance when you're actually riding, you do get rather a lot of it before you got on. You will see an official-looking booth where you pay, and you will see pictures, perhaps, of the ride in action, and plenty of evidence that people who go on come out the other end alive and with all their limbs intact, and other things that will tell you that your survival is not in question. You will see people getting off the previous ride looking happy and elated; seat belts to keep you in; and you will know that, to get a licence, the ride will have to have been tested to meet stringent safety standards. So for all the scariness that happens to you while you're on it, somewhere in the background you will have seen things that will have calmed you, and reassured you, and made you feel safe.

What makes a ride thrilling is not so much its height or the number of times you loop the loop, but the degree to which it fails to reassure you that everything will be all right. This is why rollercoaster aficionados tend to go for rickety-looking wooden rollercoasters that look like they were bodged together with old planks and nails by the homicidal hillbilly from the horror film, and which might conceivably fall apart, and why they can be sniffily dismissive of state-of-the-art steel constructions boasting 'maximum G-force travel'.

So that was one thing: in so far as the amygdala is fooled, it is temporary and incomplete, because of all of the other evidence you see that tells you it's not really dangerous. The other thing is that once you're strapped in, everything is taken care of for you – your survival doesn't rely on any particular level of skill or performance on your part: it's all done for you. It isn't very involving.

Which brings us on to the next level of playing with danger, what you might call 'dangerous sports'. 'Dangerous sports' are a very mixed bag indeed, and include everything from ancient games like boxing, wrestling and jousting to more modern inventions like freestyle motocross, base-jumping and big-wave surfing. And they most certainly include buzkashi, the national sport of Afghanistan, which, it is said, was first invented to prepare Afghan warriors to fight off the Mongol hordes of Genghis Khan.

Buzkashi involves two teams of horsemen numbering anywhere from ten or so to many hundreds; it involves a headless corpse – originally a decapitated prisoner-of-war, but now a dead calf – and it involves a 'playing field' which may be many miles long, often with a river in the middle. The game, essentially, is a pitched battle to get the body to a flag at one end of the pitch or the other. In recent years the Afghan Olympic committee has 'refined' the sport a little by outlawing knives and allowing only whips of a certain size to be used as weapons; but other than that, it's a free-for-all.

The thing about dangerous sports like buzkashi is that they are designed, among other things, to give the people who play them a real sense of danger. They do this in two ways.

The first is by doing away, as far as possible, with the corner-of-the-eye reassurance that everything is going to be all right; the second is by demanding a very high level of skill and commitment of you in order to stay safe and well, or even, in some cases, in order to stay alive.

So yes, in buzkashi, that group of men bearing down on you yelling tribal war cries really are going to knock you off your horse if you don't get out of the way pretty sharpish; and no, in freestyle motocross, that twenty-foot gap between the take-off ramp and the landing doesn't have a crash mat or a safety net in it, and you're about to attempt a double back-flip over it; and yes, in big-wave surfing, that breaker really is the size of an apartment block, and if you were to come off your board on the way down it would probably be the last thing you ever did.

All this might lead you to think that 'dangerous sports' aren't actually 'sports' at all, and that they aren't actually 'playing' at danger – they're just about danger and about taking stupid risks.

Which they would be, if you or I were just to step up and attempt, say, a double back-flip on a motocross bike or something equivalent to it.

But the interesting thing about 'dangerous sports' is that they aren't actually as dangerous as you might think, for the people who do them; and in many ways they actually have a lot more in common with rollercoasters than with the self-harming recklessness they resemble to an uninitiated outsider.

Contrariwise, sports that aren't meant to revolve

around danger at all often end up causing more inj
and even more deaths, than the 'dangerous' ones.

In the UK, for example, the most dangerous sport of
all – it kills somewhere between seven and ten participants every year – is angling. You're near water, you see,
and when you're near water there's always a chance of
falling in, and people do, and some of them die because
of it.[60]

And even if you're looking at injuries rather than
deaths, it's often the most unlikely sports that cause the
most. In America, for example, 400,000 people a year are
taken to casualty units and emergency rooms for injuries
sustained playing American football – which seems about
right, given that it is a brutal contact sport played by
six-foot-plus 'jocks' while nubile cheerleaders do distract-
ing formation acrobatics on the touchlines (which itself
results in some 20,000 injuries a year). But it turns out
that many more injuries are caused by basketball – a highly
skilful non-contact sport where you're not even supposed
to touch your opponent, much less shoulder-barge him
into the middle of next week. Non-contact basketball
causes more than 500,000 injuries requiring hospital
attention every year. That's 100,000 more than American
football. And golf, bizarrely, hospitalizes nearly 50,000
people a year, compared with 35,000 for roller-skaters and

33,000 for wrestlers. It's unfit people spraining things, apparently, in golf, and putting their backs out. That and falling out of motorized golf buggies. And being whacked with clubs, accidentally.[61]

But to return to 'dangerous sports' in the sense of sports of which danger is the point, rather than an unintended side-effect, the truth is that most of them aren't anywhere near so dangerous at all, for people who know what they're doing, as they appear to be to outsiders looking in; and the injury statistics bear this out.

Even in those dangerous sports where injuries could be described as common, such injuries tend to be relatively minor ones of a kind that the participants choose to accept, and are comfortable or even proud to live with; a price they are prepared to pay for the pleasure they get from their sport, and the badge they wear that shows what they do.

So, many boxers are happy to sport a distinctive-looking nose, but will think twice about running the risk of permanent brain damage; and many surfers and buzkashi players will push themselves in ways that mean they end up with scars that they can use to illustrate the stories of their bravery and their adventures, but not, generally, in ways that could leave them crippled for life.

What these sports do, is strip away most of the external safety measures that you can see – the crash barriers and the rails and the safety mats – and they replace them with internal safety measures that you can feel within yourself.

So whereas when you get on a rollercoaster you know that you will survive the ride because of the sturdy rails and the properly tested and well-constructed carts, in dangerous sports it's the things you've constructed inside you that see you through and make it safe to do what you do.

It's your skill, your judgement and your knowledge of your equipment; and, when these things have been painstakingly built up over many years and tested, double-tested and triple-tested, day in and day out, and when each step and building-block of every single manoeuvre has been gone through time and time again, and all of the potential pitfalls analysed and guarded against, and when there are emergency strategies in place for everything that might conceivably go wrong at any stage, then manoeuvres that look like sheer madness to outsiders, like risk taking of the most foolhardy and suicidal kind, are actually as well-planned and constructed, and in many ways as safe, as if the whole thing were running on rails.

If you look at the picture overleaf, you might be tempted to disagree. What it shows is a mountain-biker by the name of Dave Watson jumping some forty-five feet off a high cliff and over a road on which riders from the mountain stage of the Tour de France are travelling. What it doesn't show is what happened when he landed. What happened when he landed was that he crashed. Now that, you might think, is a very stupid thing to do. Spectacular, maybe, but stupid nevertheless.

More than this, he hadn't practised the jump before or even made what you might consider to be basic preparations such as riding down to the take-off point a few times at full speed, to get a feeling for what he was about to let himself in for. He didn't do this because it might have alerted the Tour de France security people, and he would have been escorted from the area and possibly charged with something. So you'd think that he might have decided not to do it, wouldn't you? All things considered. Just for a moment, imagine yourself doing what he did, right now. You push your bike right up to the top of the hill, you get on, point yourself down towards this huge great cliff that you've not even had the chance to check out properly (not that it would make much difference in my case if I had), and you pedal straight at it. You just wouldn't do it, would you? Well, I wouldn't, anyway.

But what's dangerous for you and me isn't always the same as what's dangerous for other people with different

skills. This particular mountain biker had done rather a lot of jumps over the years, starting off small and working his way up to bigger and bigger ones; and he'd crashed a bit from time to time, learnt about falling, and he felt that this particular jump was well within his capabilities. So off he went. A last-minute touch on the brakes to control his speed turned out to have been a mistake: he cleared the road but came up a bit short, and clipped the edge of the verge with his back wheel as he came in to land, and this sent him flying over the handlebars. But rather than going *splat!* face-first into the ground and ending up dead or crippled, as you or I would have done, he switched instantly to an alternative landing plan which involved rolling and bouncing, and ended up with little more than a few cuts and bruises. Oh, and a partially separated shoulder, but you'd get that falling out of a golf cart.

But because the appearance of danger in these sports is so convincing, and because there is little or nothing in the way of corner-of-the-eye reassurance, and because the level of physical and mental involvement is so high, the feelings of fear you go through can be very powerful indeed – as is the 'high' that follows.

And this 'high', while it lasts, is good. But the thing is, it doesn't last. Nor can you continually get it back by doing the same thing over and over again: the more you do it, the more familiar and 'safe' it becomes, the less fear you feel, the less of a 'rush' you will get from it. And this means that if you want to experience that rush once more, you will need to try something harder, and push further towards the limits of your fear, which means going higher, or faster, or generally being more audacious than you've ever been before. It's a continual ratcheting-up of danger to get the feeling back. It means going for a back-flip off the cliff, instead of just riding off it, and then a double back-flip, and so on until your nerve and ability begin to go back-wards with age, or until you reach a point where something scares you so badly that you realize you can go no further.

Or on the other hand, you may not want to go that way at all. You may be far less interested in jumping off cliffs and other ways of scaring yourself – with or without any kind of back-flip thrown in – and you may be far more interested in just living your life as enjoyably and as safely as possible.

So let's take a look at that right now.

PART FIVE

HOW TO LIVE DANGEROUSLY

THE DANGERS OF SAFETY

Think you understand safety and danger now? Here's a quiz for you, to see how well you're doing. You have just been offered a new job at a company two and a half miles from your home. The only way to get there is via a busy road that's packed with rush-hour traffic morning and evening, with the occasional heavy lorry. You have to decide the best and safest way to commute. There is no pavement by the side of this road, so you can't walk, but you own both a bicycle and a car. You've heard that there have been one or two fatal accidents on the road in recent years involving cyclists. No motorists have been killed during the same period. Just to be absolutely sure of your facts, you've done some research, and you've discovered that on average, according to the British Medical Association,[62] cycling in traffic carries a risk of death and serious injury eleven times greater than making the same journey by car.

So, which is the safer way to get to work and back each day: by car or by bike?

And that's where you're wrong. The safest way to make that journey each day is actually to go by bike. Even though there is a greater risk of being killed in an accident, your life expectancy will be significantly higher if you cycle.

Here's why. Do you remember that question from earlier about which kills more people, accident or disease, and it turned out that disease kills many times more? Well, that's why you're better off cycling. You see, although cyclists are more likely to die in road accidents than motorists, road accidents account for only 1.4 per cent of all deaths whereas heart and lung diseases account for over 50 per cent of all deaths; and heart disease in particular finishes off a third of us. People who cycle twenty-five miles a week – that's five miles a day, five days a week – halve their risk of getting heart disease. And that means that far more cyclists' lives are extended by the exercise than are cut short by the accidents.

A study of actuarial data carried out by Mayer Hillman (again) for the British Medical Association[63] found that the years of life gained through improved fitness due to regular cycling outweigh the years lost in cycling accidents by twenty to one. Which is to say, for every year of life lost through cycling accidents, twenty are gained.

Hillman's data included a survey of 9,000 male civil

servants which found that the 9 per cent who cycled regularly, or did other similarly vigorous exercise, were less likely to suffer coronary heart disease than other men. Another survey of 1,400 factory workers found that there was a direct and significant link between regular cycling and overall health and fitness, such that regular cyclists were five years younger, in health terms, than those who cycled occasionally, and ten years younger than those who didn't cycle at all.

The only way that motorists can increase their life expectancy to match those of the cyclists they whizz past is by doing an equivalent amount of regular physical exercise. Which, with the best will in the world, few people do. We may want to, and we may have the best of intentions; we may even splash out on a gym membership after the excesses of Christmas, but what with work, family and other commitments, the membership card often ends up buried at the bottom of a drawer until it expires the following December. That's how many gyms make their money.

So that's your answer: cycling is safer than driving, despite the risk of accident. Now here's a bonus question. Imagine that you have decided to cycle to work on this busy road. Do you think it might be a good idea, from the point of view of safety, to wear a proper, well-fitted cycling helmet, or do you think you'd be better off without one? Here's a hint: most cyclists who are killed in road accidents die of head injuries.

And you're wrong again. Bizarre as it may seem, all the evidence says that you'd be safer without one.

Let's work this one through, to see why, and let's start by looking at what cycle helmets do, and what they are for.

The first thing to say is that cycle helmets do protect you in the event of a fall. And I ought to declare an interest here, on account of the fact that I've fallen on my head enough times, both with and without a helmet on, to qualify as a . . . I was going to say 'test pilot' but 'crash-test dummy' is probably more accurate. Falling on your head a lot is not big, and it's certainly not clever. It also probably accounts, to an extent, for the way this book has turned out.

Anyway, I fell off my bike when I was a child, unhelmeted and shirtless, and was knocked unconscious in the road (as well as being horribly grazed). Since growing up and wearing a helmet, I've been knocked out cold twice after falling off of a skateboard. Perhaps it's even three times. Do you know, I don't actually know. It's definitely at least two, and I have a strong suspicion that it's three, but I can't exactly remember. That's a bit shocking, isn't it? You ought to be able to remember something like that, but for some reason I can't. Anyway, as well as the two (or three) complete knockouts – and the consequent waking up on the ground surrounded by people, and wondering where I was and how I got there, and having tunnel-vision for hours afterward, and being so dazed and stupid that I didn't realize it was a bad idea to get into my car and drive home, and then keeping on repeating myself all the time – I've had a few more falls, wearing a helmet, that didn't knock me out, but that I'm convinced would have, or worse, otherwise. Once I hit my head on concrete while wearing a fibreglass helmet, and got up to find the helmet split and embedded with stones. That could have been my head. And once I went over the handlebars of my mountain bike, landed on boulders face-first and broke the jaw-guard of the full-face crash helmet I was wearing, but got up completely uninjured. And I know it's not comparing like with like, but the time I was knocked out without wearing a helmet I was out for longer, because I woke up in someone's house: they'd picked me up and taken me indoors, and I'd been there for some time before I came round.

So cycle helmets (and skateboard helmets, which are similar), as I can tell you from personal experience, work pretty well. The sort of fall they are designed to cope with is the sort of fall you have when you lose control of your bike and hit the ground up to a speed of around 12 miles per hour. And the sort of injury they protect you against is the sort of injury I had falling off my bike unprotected as a child, which is to say low-severity, short-term concussion. These types of injuries are unpleasant if they happen to you, and distressing if they happen to your child, but they aren't usually serious. I survived mine with no long-term ill effects, even though someone had to come and pick me up off the road unconscious. In fact, only a very small minority – no more than 2 per cent – of those kinds of cycle injuries are ever severe or critical. So cycle helmets are very good for reducing the impact of non-serious injuries for the kinds of people who are likely to lose control and fall off their bikes,[64] which is children, generally, and people who are old enough to know better but who persist in trying to do tricks and stunts when they ought to have grown out of it.

However – and it's a big however – most of the 200 or so people who die in cycle accidents every year aren't children or ageing thrill-seekers. They are normal adults riding on public roads who are hit by cars or lorries. And in 83 per cent of cases they're hit through no fault of their own.

Being hit by several tons of metal at speed is the kind

of accident against which a cycle helmet gives you no protection whatsoever. Motorcyclists aren't much better off, since their helmets offer a lot less protection than you might think, too: even Darth Vader wouldn't survive a direct hit against a solid object at more than 15 miles per hour.

So if you ride to work on the busy road we talked about, wearing a crash helmet won't do a thing to save your life in the event of a collision with a car or a lorry.

That may come as a surprise to you. It does to most people. You see, most people who wear a helmet imagine – quite reasonably – that it will in some way make their journey safer. Because they believe this they feel a little less vulnerable than they would if they weren't wearing one, so they are slightly more likely to ride aggressively or recklessly.[65] Drivers, meanwhile, seeing cyclists 'protected' by helmets, take slightly less care when passing them: according to research, they drive, on average, 3.35 inches closer to a cyclist wearing a helmet, and come within 3 feet 23 per cent more often.[66] All of this means that cyclists in helmets are slightly more likely to become one of the thirty-odd cyclists a year who die in traffic accidents caused by their own bad or careless cycling.[67]

There is a parallel in motorcycling, too. In Britain, in the years following the introduction of compulsory helmet legislation, the number of pedestrians killed in collisions with motorcycles increased, suggesting that riders, feeling more confident, drove more recklessly.

So there you have it. The safest way to get from your home to your new workplace down a busy road on which cyclists have been killed is on your bike. Without a helmet.

Oh – I also meant to say, earlier on, when I was listing my tally of Head Injuries I Have Suffered, that I have also been a victim of fishing – which, as we established earlier, is Britain's most dangerous sport. Standing on Southend pier as a child, watching my fishing rod, some imbecile took a big swing with his rod to cast his line out into the sea without checking to see if there was anyone standing near by. Of course there *was* someone standing near by, and that someone was me. The first I knew of it, a lead weight cracked me on the head and then, an instant later, a hook with a big fat lugworm wriggling on it embedded itself in my cheek. My life wasn't endangered, like those of the eight or ten anglers who are killed each year, but I wasn't very happy about it even so. None of which has anything at all to do with the risks of cycling, but I just felt the need to get it off of my chest, set it down on record, because it's been bothering me. Although probably if I'd been wearing a helmet of some kind, on the off-chance, I might have been safer.

Which brings us neatly back to the safety or otherwise of cycle helmets for children. Because although wearing a helmet will protect them from the kinds of non-serious, non-life-threatening injuries they are likely to get on their bikes, studies have shown that children are actually between two and three times more likely to suffer those kinds of head injuries while climbing or jumping than while cycling.[68] So perhaps they should wear helmets when they go out to play, or just all the time, just in case. Or else they should just ride their bikes like previous generations did, without their parents fussing and agonizing so much over them, and take whatever lumps and bumps come their way as a normal part of childhood, to teach them what sorts of things in life hurt, and to learn how best to avoid them in the future.

In fact, and while we're on the subject, now is a very good time to look at today's 'concerned' parenting, and what its long-term consequences might be for the development and safety of the children it sets out to protect.

Do you remember the knock on the door, and your mum opening it to find little Johnny or Jenny from round the corner asking if you were coming out to play? That isn't how things are done any more. For one thing, going to call for a friend unsupervised might involve crossing a road, and this is something that fewer and fewer parents are prepared to allow their children to do. According to research by the Department of Transport, the proportion of children aged seven to ten who are not allowed to cross the road unsupervised rose from one in five (22 per cent) in 2002 to one in two (49 per cent) in 2006. Instead, small children stay indoors until or unless an activity is laid on for them – a class or a course, say – or a 'play-date' is arranged by the parents. A 'play-date' involves one or more sets of parents loading their offspring into a vehicle and delivering them to the house of another child, where adult-supervised play occurs.[69]

There are two kinds of adverse consequences to this way of living: physical and psychological.

Children who stay indoors and never go out to play don't get as much exercise as they should. By the age of eleven, only one boy in twenty and only one girl in 250 takes the amount of exercise they need to keep fit, according to a study published in 2007 by researchers at Bristol and Bath universities.[70] What happens when children don't take enough exercise is that they become fat, among other things. At the time of writing, 10 per cent of all British under-tens, and a quarter of all British eleven-to fifteen-year-olds are classified as clinically obese. At the current rate of increase, the British government estimate that by 2050 almost half of all children will be dangerously overweight, unless drastic action is taken. And being fat not only looks bad, but it can dramatically worsen your health and shorten your life expectancy, too.[71]

Being fat can make you diabetic. In recent years, the medical profession has had to rename 'adult-onset diabetes' as 'type-2 diabetes' because of the growing number of children and young people suffering from it.

It can give you high blood pressure, too, which in turn can lead to heart attacks, heart failure, strokes and kidney disease in later life. The incidence of high blood pressure in young people in Britain has doubled in the past twenty years, and by the time they reach their twenties, a quarter of British men are at or above the 140 mm of mercury systolic blood-pressure threshold for adult hypertension. Which is another way of saying they have high blood pressure. The typical age at which high blood pressure shifts from just being something that can be measured to being something that causes you to be ill used to be around fifty. Now, increasingly, it's between twenty-five and thirty.[72]

That's what not going out, and sitting around on your backside watching the television or playing computer games does for you.

Another thing that happens, besides getting fat, is that you don't get as dirty, or have as much contact with germs, as you would if you went out without your parents watching you and spent time playing unsupervised in places where you really ought not to be, doing things your parents wouldn't want you to do. And the home itself is getting cleaner and more hygienic, what with antibacterial wipes and sprays and cutting-boards and whatever else, and what with antibiotics being doled out at the first sign of a sniffle, and what with the fact that six out of ten people now believe that children 'should be protected from all bacteria'.[73] And the problem with all this is that it stops children's immune systems developing properly, which means that they end up with less resistance to disease in later life and – according to some authorities – with a much higher incidence of allergies.[74]

So those are some of the physical problems that you will cause your children to suffer if you don't let them go out to play. But there are mental ones as well.

People who know about this sort of thing have been getting themselves quite worked up about what overprotective parenting is doing to children's mental development, from the Mental Health Foundation report in 1999[75] which concluded that 'There are risks to children in insulating them and not letting them develop their own coping mechanisms, or do things their own way' to the three hundred or so of the great and good who signed an open letter in 2007 warning that the loss of opportunities for independent, outdoor play is 'a major factor in the rise of mental health problems in recent years'.

These notables included sixty psychologists and psychotherapists, more than forty university professors, the leaders of British teaching unions and children's charities, plus a sprinkling of well-known authors and child-care experts thrown in for good measure.

The gist of their argument was that not letting children make their own decisions, not letting them play outside unsupervised, not letting them travel alone and not letting them take responsibility for their own safety and wellbeing means that they don't learn how to do these things properly, and they grow up powerless and unhappy, and deficient in what ought to be basic life skills. '"Real play",' the letter says, '– socially interactive, first-hand, loosely supervised, has always been a vital part of children's development, and its loss could have serious implications.' As to what those 'serious implications' might be, the letter goes on to talk about a 'mental health crisis'. That can't be good.[76]

And as if that weren't enough, there have also been all

sorts of studies of monkeys and other species that show time and time again that primates kept in captivity and deprived of freedom and rough-and-tumble play in their youth develop into incompetent adults.

Happy or not, and facing a mental health crisis or not, when children who have never learnt how to handle danger on their own do eventually get their freedom at fifteen or sixteen, they end up taking stupid risks – witness the recent craze for 'tombstoning', which is jumping off cliffs and piers and hoping that you land in the sea, rather than on the rocks below, and train-surfing, which is standing on the roof of a speeding train. Or else, if they're 'good' teenagers, and not the kind to take stupid risks, they end up being so timid that they miss out on the opportunities of life. Either way, because few of them were allowed to cross roads unaided when they were younger, their road sense is not all it should be. As a result, the proportion of teenage road-accident victims as a percentage of the whole has risen steeply in recent years.[77]

Nor should we forget the parents in all of this, and the effects on them. All of this worrying and supervising, you see, and all of this constantly being responsible for their children's safety and wellbeing, doesn't come without a cost.

There's the investment in time, to start with. Parents today spend around four times as much time looking after their children than their own parents spent in 1975.[78] And then there's all the ferrying to and fro that goes on: over 900 million hours a year, on average, are being spent by parents escorting their children to places to which, in many instances, they ought to be perfectly capable of going on their own.

But beyond the time there's the stress and the worry, and what that does to you. Parents – and mothers in particular, on whom the bulk of the burden falls – who are too scared of traffic and 'stranger danger' to leave their children unattended even for a few hours during the school holidays don't actually have a very nice time of it. For some, it all gets to be too much. In recent years, alcoholism treatment centres have experienced major increases in the admission of women – with the peaks occurring during the school holidays, when the pressure of constantly looking after children is at its most intense.[79]

A lot of these women say that the reason they feel the way they do, and the reason they feel unable to cope, is the strain of having to provide constant entertainment for their children and never having a moment to themselves, or a moment when they can just send the children off to the park, or out into the street to go and find something to do. Some of the wealthier ones manage to offload their children to a string of well-supervised and worthy-sounding 'educational summer camps', to get them out of the way, but the rest of the mothers are stuck with having to organize their lives around their children, with no break, for weeks on end; and after a while it all becomes too much.

There's something of a theme in these bike-or car, protect-or-neglect decisions, and it is this: we over-estimate, massively, the risk of a sudden, violent event on the roads or at the hands of a stranger, and we under-estimate, to a shocking degree, the very real risks to our health, our wellbeing and our sanity that we bring upon ourselves in our attempts to avoid everything that we imagine to be 'dangerous'.

To put it another way: the more we try to avoid danger, the more dangerous life becomes.

And it's not even very much fun, living like that.

So, if avoiding danger doesn't keep us safe, what does? That's what we're going to look at next.

THE SAFETY OF DANGER

Winter is not a pleasant time for drivers. The nights are long and dark, conditions are often slippery and unpredictable and liable to cause you to crash. And yet the biggest dips in the number of people killed on the roads actually come then, in the winter, at the times when the road conditions are at their very worst. The reason for this is that drivers slow down and take more care, precisely because the roads seem so dangerous.

Another little story, also to do with roads and driving: in the 1960s, the Swedes switched from driving on the left-hand side of the road to driving on the right. During the changeover, the number of traffic accidents fell by 17 per cent. The reason was that the roads felt less familiar, less safe. And just as they do on icy roads in the dead of winter, drivers slowed down and took more care.[80]

Where this is all leading is to one of the most important theories of how human beings deal with danger and risk, and why. It's a theory that has very important and far-reaching implications, as we'll see a little later. The theory goes by a number of names, including 'risk homeostasis theory'[81] and 'risk compensation theory', but you may prefer to think of it as just plain common sense.

Here's what the theory says: all of us have a natural or 'ideal' level of risk that we feel comfortable with in our lives. Your level may be different from my level, and both our levels may be different from Genghis Khan's, on account of risk-taking genes, testosterone and all the other factors we talked about a while back; but whoever we are and whatever we're like, we're all looking for the 'right' level of risk, and the 'right' balance between safety and excitement. When things become more dangerous than we like, we take more precautions – when the roads are icy, for example. And – here's the important part – when things become noticeably safer, we feel that it's all right to take a few more risks.

So, strange as it may seem, and mad as it may seem, and hard to believe as it may seem, the safest course of action, much of the time, is the one that appears, on the face of it, the most dangerous.

In 1989, the year that UK law first required children in the rear seats of cars to wear seat belts, the number of children killed and injured in rear seats didn't go down at all. It didn't even stay the same. What it did was ~~actually increased. Significantly.~~ ally increased. Significantly. The reason for this was that people felt their children were now properly protected, so they didn't have to worry so much, and so they could afford to drive faster and more recklessly.

And when, for example, we make children's playgrounds less dangerous by replacing tarmac with special spongy rubber stuff, and when we take away the big tall slides and climbing frames, and when we prevent children from playing conkers unless they wear protective goggles, what we are doing is not actually making them any safer: we are just making life duller, and challenging children's ingenuity to come up with ways of experiencing the same level of thrills that the old playgrounds used to give them, and that the old unstructured play used to give them. Which may mean using playgrounds in ways for which they were never intended – as places to vandalize and spray graffiti on, for example, which carries the risk of being chased by an irate adult – or not using them at all but going somewhere else altogether – a derelict building, say, or a railway line you can run across as a train approaches, and getting your thrills there instead.

In the 1990s a committee of scientists, psychologists and health-and-safety experts from sixteen countries

evidence for this theory, to see
..ecautions actually protect people,
, just make them feel safe and confident
..o take bigger risks. Their verdict was unanimous
..d unequivocal: 'It is clear,' they said, 'that confidence in safety devices – whether they be helmets, seat belts, safety ropes for climbers, or safety nets for trapeze artists – affects behaviour. People respond in a way that tends to nullify the intended effect of the device. Safety measures that ignore this tendency almost always disappoint their promoters.'[82]

And here's the point: if it isn't so much things themselves that cause accidents as people's willingness to take risks, then making things safer won't mean there will be fewer accidents. It just means that there will be different ones.

The only real way to make people safer, the only real way to cut the rate of accidents in one place without it leading to more accidents happening somewhere else, is to lower people's willingness to take the particular risk that you have in mind. Which is to say, it is to make that risk more frightening.

Or, to put it another way, the most effective way to make a thing safer is to make it more dangerous.

*

The best way to illustrate that point is with two examples, one about dangerous roads, and the other about dangerous playgrounds.

For as long as there has been traffic on the roads, and accidents caused by that traffic, people have believed that the way to make roads safer is by putting more safety measures in place: things like traffic lights, road signs, lane markings, pedestrian crossings and, on particularly busy roads, steel or concrete barriers to keep the people in cars and the people on foot separated from each other.

But in the late 1970s a Dutch traffic engineer by the name of Hans Monderman[83] began to develop a radically different way of doing things. Appointed as the traffic safety officer of the province of Friesland, he began by incorporating traffic-calming features into roads – things like road narrowings, strategically placed trees and flower-beds to discourage people from speeding. The more of this he did, the more he came to believe that the answer lay less in the structure of the roads themselves than in the minds of the drivers who used them. It was then that a radical idea struck him: that the biggest impact of all would come not from adding new safety features, but from taking every last one of them away. This would mean, he said, stripping out everything designed to keep people safe, and everything designed to tell people what they ought to be doing: so, no road signs, no barriers, no separation at all between the road and the pavement, even. Pedestrians and drivers alike would have to share the roads on equal terms, and take personal responsibility for their own safety. 'We're losing our capacity for socially responsible behaviour,' Monderman said. 'The greater the number of prescriptions, the more people's sense of personal responsibility dwindles.'

He presented his ideas to the Dutch government, who initially were less than impressed. But he persisted, and eventually he was given permission for a limited trial in a small village, whose residents had previously complained that it had become a daily thoroughfare for 6,000 speeding cars. Monderman stripped out anything and everything that could be remotely considered a 'safety feature'. Within two weeks, speeds on the road had dropped by more than half and the residents were delighted.

Time passed, and more small-scale experiments proved successful. The Monderman approach acquired a name: 'shared space'. And then, in 2003, came the idea's first big test: the city of Drachten. Exactly as in the test villages, all traffic lights and signs were removed from the city centre, apart from a single sign at the boundary saying 'Verkeersbordvrij', which means 'free of traffic signs' in Dutch.

Until that time, Drachten city centre had an ave of eight accidents per year. Since the new system was introduced, there has been none at all. In addition, and despite the fact that the town's main junction handles 22,000 cars a day, traffic jams now almost never happen.

What does happen, in Monderman's words, is that 'When you don't exactly know who has right of way, you tend to seek eye contact with other road users . . . You automatically reduce your speed, you have contact with other people and you take greater care.'

Since 2003, shared-space schemes have been set up around the world.

In London's Kensington High Street, all the barriers, signs and markings have been taken away, as a result of which average traffic speeds have reduced and the number of road casualties has fallen, from seventy-one in the year before the scheme to forty in the year afterwards.

And this seems to have been repeated everywhere the scheme has been tried, whether in Holland, in Haslach and Wolfach in Germany, in Norrköping in Sweden, or in Palm Beach in Florida.

A dangerous road, it seems, is a safe road.

Now let's look at playgrounds.

People worry about playgrounds, and how dangerous

they are – or how dangerous they appear to be. Children can, and do, get hurt playing in playgrounds: statistically speaking, if you were to pay regular visits to your local playground throughout your childhood up to the age of sixteen, you would sustain an average of one injury. But the chances are that it would be a minor one, something along the lines of a grazed knee with gravel in it. In order to sustain a 'proper' injury – a broken bone or the like – requiring a trip to A&E, that would take you, on average, 200 years. Or, to put it another way, every year, one in every 200 children has to go to hospital to be patched up. It's even possible to kill yourself in a playground. But it's just not very likely. For the average child, it would take 30 million years. So playgrounds aren't particularly dangerous, as places to play go. But that hasn't stopped parents fussing and fretting, and councils laying down rubber matting and ripping out anything remotely enjoyable, for 'health and safety' reasons. In the ten years from 1990 to 2000, they spent somewhere between £200–300 million of your money on that.[84]

And if regular swings-and-slide playgrounds have fallen foul of the health-and-safety fanatics, then you can imagine what has happened to the places we used to call 'adventure playgrounds'.

If you've not come across an adventure playground –
and if you're below a certain age you might not have come
across one before because there aren't very many of them
around now – it is (or was) a loosely supervised collection
of rope-swings, ladders and platforms that offer what has
been described as 'opportunities to test skills appropriate
to chimpanzees'. A lot of the obstacles are made of old
telegraph poles, planks and ropes.

In 1985, a geographer by the name of John G. U. Adams
decided to take a look at these adventure playgrounds,
perhaps to give himself a break from writing about oxbow
lakes and terminal moraines all the time, and memorizing
capital cities in order to fill in the gaps on maps correctly.

What Adams found, standing there with his clipboard
and his pen, in his corduroy jacket with leather patches
on the elbows, was three things. One was that the accident
rate in adventure playgrounds was lower than in nice,
safe playgrounds with rubberized matting and smooth
surfaces. Another was that in adventure playgrounds
there was a lot less vandalism and hooliganism, perhaps
as a consequence of less boredom. And the third thing
he found was that because the accident rate and the
vandalism rate were so much lower than in 'normal'
playgrounds, the insurance companies charged them
lower premiums.[85] Which is significant, because insurance

companies aren't in the business of giving away money if they can help it.

But because adventure playgrounds look too dangerous for modern sensibilities, they have largely been replaced by the 'safe' kind, where you get more accidents and more vandalism.

In Scandinavia, however, although the tide of opinion is moving in the direction of 'safety', it is still possible to swim against it, at least as far as playgrounds are concerned.

Asbjorn Flemmen, a headmaster in Skudenshavn, Norway, has recently designed a playground for his school that probably would never even have been countenanced elsewhere, and, if he'd ever attempted to build it, would have had health-and-safety officers swarming all over it, spouting instructions to change this and supervise that, and put in fences here and crash mats there, and to provide proper protective equipment for the children – if they'd ever been allowed to use it. It's a kind of school playground, you see, that actively encourages dangerous 'thrill-seeking'.[86]

There are two things that make it dangerous: one is the kind of thing to be found there: a 'jungle' area left to grow wild, a 'hide-and-seek area' that children can disappear into, and all sorts of heavy and potentially hazardous hut-building materials, all left lying around for children to do what they want with, without any official guidance or instruction at all. The other thing is that there are no adults around, whether to help in the event of an accident or to spot and act on bullying or illicit activities. Adults are advised to back off and stay out at all times.

Even for the famously permissive Scandinavians this was considered a bit much at the start, and people complained and predicted a *Lord of the Flies* sort of situation – or whatever the Norwegian equivalent is. And they were proven right – or so they thought when pretty much straight away there were two broken arms, a broken leg and all sorts of cuts and bruises. In Britain, as in many other Western countries, that would have been it; Social Services would have been called in, the school closed down and Mr Flemmen carted off by the police. But in Norway none of this happened, and the experiment was allowed to continue. And what happened next was really interesting. What happened next was that the injuries dried up to a trickle, and then stopped. No more broken bones, no more gashes, no more concussions. The children, through experiencing danger, and after seeing what happened to people who didn't take enough care, soon came to appreciate their own limitations.

And despite concerns from worried parents and anti-bullying professionals, bullying didn't spiral out of control, either. It's not to say that there weren't arguments and flare-ups, but the children seemed to have learnt how to resolve these conflicts of their own accord and without resorting to murder.

But quite apart from the absence of injury and the absence of bullying, it was perhaps the positive benefits to the children that were the most striking. Not only had the children learnt to cope with danger and conflict, but they had developed physically and mentally to the extent that their improved levels of fitness, physical mobility and social skills stunned both parents and teachers.

Danger, it seems, really is better for you, most of the time, than safety.

LIVING DANGEROUSLY

The world is full of risks.

There are all sorts of things out there that, if you let them, could end up killing or maiming you or your family.

That's why you feel fear when danger is near. Fear helps you. It keeps you safe.

It's not perfect, though, fear. Sometimes you don't feel it when perhaps you ought to – for example, when you are faced with things that seem harmless at the time, and continue to seem harmless, in your direct experience, for day after day and year after year, but then end up killing you gradually – asbestos, say, or cigarettes.

And sometimes – too often, these days – we feel fear when really we oughtn't, and we imagine all sorts of terrors and perils lurking on every corner that either don't exist at all or are about as likely to happen to you or to anyone you know as being struck down by a comet, or eaten by an escaped rhinoceros.

We get it wrong because of the way our brains are made, and because we see and 'experience' so many perils and disasters so often and so intensely on the television and in the newspapers, and, lately, on the Internet that we come to believe, quite mistakenly, that they're likely to happen to us, or to people we know and love, and that sends us into a panic.

As a result, we take all sorts of unnecessary and restrictive precautions, and we collude and go meekly along with the people who rule our lives by passing and enforcing all sorts of pointless and infantile rules and regulations. And because of this, we stop letting our children go out to play, and we do not stop to think how we end up damaging their physical and mental development through what we do, or to how we leave them a legacy that will shorten their lives through letting them get fat and unfit.

Perhaps at some time in the future people will look back at what we have done, and how we have chosen to live our lives, and they will shake their heads in amazement. But we can't wait until then: none of us can. There is so much that needs to be done, and so little time left to do it in. When you see the speed at which so much of your life has gone by already, and when you think about the speed with which the rest of it will go, and when it suddenly strikes you, quite unexpectedly, in an unguarded moment – while washing the dishes, say, or pausing a moment, reading in your chair and looking up to see dust swirling in a shaft of sunlight from the window – when the fact of it hits you, and the knowledge of the presence of death all around us, it draws you up short. Life is here and now, and then it is gone.

And, while it is here, fear is here to help us live it.

If you really want to live your life to the full, and if you want to do and see and feel all that it has to offer, then you need to push at your fear, to see how far it will let you go, and when and why and how it will let you do what you want. In return, it will push back at you, and you need to be prepared to give, and to bend to its will. And when it says, 'This far and no further,' and means it, sometimes you just have to stop, no matter how much you might want to do otherwise. If you do that, in the end you and fear will get to know and trust each other, and learn how to rub along together just fine: and at that point you will know what it means to really live, and to live dangerously.

NOTES

1 'Hurling sweets at panto "too risky for children"', *Daily Telegraph*, 7 December 2007.
2 Marsh & McLennan.
3 ICM Poll, *Guardian*, 16 August 2000.
4 'The Worry Report', BUPA 2007.
5 'Phobias "dominating the daily lives of millions"', *Daily Telegraph*, 7 October 2007.
6 'McDonald's targeted in obesity lawsuit', BBC News, 22 November 2002.
7 'Big jury award for coffee burn', *New York Times*, 19 August 1994.
8 'Woman loses skylight fall claim', BBC News, 28 March 2007.
9 'Damage claim for £2m loss gambler', BBC News, 27 February 2008; 'Compulsive gambler Graham Calvert loses High Court claim against William Hill', *The Times*, 10 March 2008.
10 See *Junk Medicine: Doctors, Lies and the Addiction Bureaucracy*, Theodore Dalrymple, Harriman House Publishing, August 2007.
11 'Fat people are just greedy, says BMA chief', *Daily Telegraph*, 3 August 2007 and 'Obese? That's because you eat too much, says top doctor', *Daily Mail*, 17 September 2007.
12 'Outrage over the ban that shouldn't happen to a vet', *The Times*, 2 August 2007.
13 'A&E units "stretched" as child patients rise', *Daily Telegraph*, 8 August 2007.
14 *Playing it Safe: The Crazy World of Britain's Health and Safety Regulations*, Alan Pearce, The Friday Project, 2007.
15 'Council erects danger sign: "Warning falling pears"', *Daily Mail*, 3 October 2006.

16 'The baloney over Barney', *Guardian*, 15 June 2007.

17 *Playing It Safe.*

18 'For us ze war is over by tea time, ja', *The Times*, 18 November 2007.

19 *One False Move: A Study of Children's Independent Mobility*, Mayer Hillman, John Adams and John Whitelegg, Policy Studies Institute, 1990.

20 'Rearing children in captivity', BBC News, 4 June 2007; see also 'The Good Childhood – A National Inquiry', the Children's Society 2007.

21 ChildWise Monitor Report, Winter 2004–5, www.childwise.co.uk

22 'Pupils face tracking bugs in school blazers', *Guardian*, 21 August 2007.

23 'Children in the UK', Office of National Statistics, 31 July 2002.

24 'Help! How afraid should I be of stranger danger?', *The Times*, 6 June 2007.

25 'The odds of dying from . . .' NSC, 2008: http://www.nsc.org/lrs/ statinfo/odds.htm

26 *The Polar Bear Strategy: Reflections on Risk in Modern Life*, John F. Ross, Perseus Books, 1999; 'Analysing the Daily Risks of Life', Richard Wilson, *Technology Review* 81, No. 4.

27 'Men and mowers top the new garden danger list', RoSPA press release, 28 April 2004. Figures based on the Department of Trade and Industry's Home Accident Surveillance System report.

28 *The Polar Bear Strategy: Reflections on Risk in Modern Life.*

29 'Three deaths linked to "living on air" cult', *Sunday Times*, 26 September 1999.

30 'Dietary pesticides (99.99% all-natural)', B. N. Ames, M. Profet and L. S. Gold, *Proceedings of the National Academy of Sciences*, vol. 87, October 1990; *The Polar Bear Strategy: Reflections on Risk in Modern Life.*

31 *The Polar Bear Strategy: Reflections on Risk in Modern Life.*

32 'Girl overdoses on espresso coffee', BBC News, 13 August 2007.

33 'An Unfortunate Pattern Observed on US Domestic Jet Accidents', Prof. Arnold Barnett and Todd Curtis, Massachusetts Institute of Technology, *Flight Safety Digest*, October 1991.

34 'Is flying still the safest way to travel?' BBC News, 24 August 2005.

35 *Traffic Safety and the Driver*, Leonard Evans, John Wiley & Sons, 1991.

36 *Traffic Safety and the Driver.*

37 *Traffic Safety and the Driver.*

38 'Cycle Helmets: The Case for and Against', Mayer Hillman, Policy Studies Institute, 1993.

39 'Analysing the Daily Risks of Life', Richard Wilson, *Technology Review* 81, No. 4.

40 'Risk education statistics', Health and Safety Executive, http://www. hse.gov.uk/education/statistics.htm

41 'Placing Risk Between Panic and Apathy: A New Industry Emerges', Cristine Russell, 1988, Alicia Patterson Foundation.

42 'Placing Risk Between Panic and Apathy: A New Industry Emerges'.

43 'Investment Behavior and the Negative Side of Emotion', Baba Shiv, George Loewenstein, Antoine Beechara, Hanna Damasio, Antonio R. Damasio, *Psychological Science*, June 2005.

44 *The Synaptic Self*, Joseph E. LeDoux, Macmillan 2002. Most of the neuroscience in this chapter comes from LeDoux, who is Professor of Neuroscience and Psychology at New York University and director of the Center for the Neuroscience of Fear and Anxiety.

45 'Stathmin, a Gene Enriched in the Amygdala, Controls Both Learned and Innate Fear', Vadim Y. Bolshakov, *Cell*, 18 November 2005.

46 In *The Synaptic Self*, LeDoux talks about a faster 'low road' from the amygdala and a slower 'high road' from the cortex.

47 *The Emotional Brain: The Mysterious Underpinnings of Emotional Life*, Joseph E. Ledoux, Weidenfeld & Nicolson,1998.

48 *The Expression of the Emotions in Man and Animals*, Charles Darwin, 1872.

49 'Neocortex size as a constraint on group size in primates', Robin Dunbar, *Journal of Human Evolution* 22, 1992, and 'Coevolution of neocortical size, group size and language in humans', Robin Dunbar, *Behavioral and Brain Sciences* 16 (4) 1993.

50 'Hidden Rules Often Distort Ideas of Risk', *New York Times*, 1 February 1994.

51 'Hidden Rules Often Distort Ideas of Risk', *New York Times*, 1 February 1994.

52 *The Polar Bear Strategy: Reflections on Risk in Modern Life*.

53 *A Counterblaste to Tobacco*, James I, 1604.

54 *Eccentrics*, David Joseph Weeks and Jamie James, Weidenfeld & Nicholson, 1995; and *Mango: The Life and Times of Squire John Mytton of Halston 1796–1834*, Jean Holdsworth, Dobson Books, 1972.

55 'Are You a Risk Taker?', Marvin Zuckerman, *Psychology Today*, 1 November 2000.

56 'Genghis Khan a Prolific Lover, DNA Data Implies', *National Geographic*, 14 February 2003.

57 Are You a Risk Taker?, Marvin Zuckerman.

58 Are You a Risk Taker?, Marvin Zuckerman.

59 'Octopamine modulates honey-bee dance behavior', A. B. Barron & co., Proceedings of the National Academy of Sciences (USA), November 2006. *'In mammals, dopaminergic systems mediate the learning of reward, the motivation to seek reward, and the subjective pleasurable sensations triggered by the perception of rewarding stimuli. Perhaps a role of OA in the insect brain is analogous to that of dopaminergic circuits in the mammalian forebrain.'*

60 'The World's Most Dangerous Sports', *Forbes*, 7 August 2002.

61 'The World's Most Dangerous Sports', *Forbes*, 7 August 2002.

62 *Cycling: Towards Health & Safety*, OUP, 1992.

63 *Cycling: Towards Health & Safety*, OUP, 1992.

64 'Cycle helmets: the case for and against', Mayer Hillman, Policy Studies Institute, 1993.

65 'Understanding children's injury-risk behavior: wearing safety gear can lead to increased risk taking', B. A. Morrongiello, B. Walpole and J. Lasenby, *Accident Analysis & Prevention* Volume 39, Issue 3, May 2007; and 'Risk compensation in children's activities: A pilot study', D. Mok, G. Gore, B. Hagel, E. Mok, H. Magdalinos, B. Pless, *Paediatrics and Child Health*, May/June 2004, Volume 9, Number 5.

66 'Strange but True: Helmets Attract Cars to Cyclists', *Scientific American*, 10 May 2007.

67 'Cycle helmets: the case for and against', Mayer Hillman, Policy Studies Institute, 1993.

68 'Cycle helmets: the case for and against'.

69 'Careful parents may cost lives', *The Times*, 11 September 2007.

70 'Only one in 250 girls takes enough exercise', *Daily Telegraph*, 17 September 2007 (report of findings of ALSPAC – Avon Longitudinal Study of Parents and Children, headed by Professor Chris Riddoch, of Bath University).

71 'Half of all boys will be obese, warns leaked report', *Observer*, 29 July 2007.

72 'Children under pressure: an underestimated burden?', Saverio

Stranges & Francesco P. Cappucio, Warwick Medical School, *British Medical Journal*, 92, April 2007.

73 '"Playstation generation" have poor immune systems', *Daily Mail*, 25 September 2007 (report of ICM poll, with comment by Professor Ken Jones, an immunologist at Cardiff School of Health Sciences).

74 'Link from hygiene to allergies gains support', *Nature*, 25 March 2004.

75 *Rethinking Risk and the Precautionary Principle*, ed. Julian Morris, Butterworth-Heinemann, 2000.

76 'No outdoor play "hurts children"', BBC News, 10 September 2007.

77 'The Older Child Pedestrian Casualty', Carole Millar Research, Scottish Government Publications 1998 and *THINK! 2007/08 Strategy*, Department for Transport.

78 *No Fear: Growing up in a risk averse society*, Tim Gill, Calouste Gulbenkian Foundation, October 2007.

79 'Of course mothers are driven to drink', *Daily Telegraph*, 4 August 2007.

80 *Why Things Bite Back*, Edward Tenner, Alfred A. Knopf, 1996.

81 *Target Risk 2: A New Psychology of Safety and Health*, Gerald J. S. Wilde, PDE Publications. Full book available online at http://psyc.queensu.ca/target/index.html

82 *Behavioural Adaptations to Changes in the Road Transport System*, OECD, 1990.

83 'A Path to Road Safety With No Signposts', *New York Times*, 22 January 2005; Hans Monderman's obituary, *Guardian*, 2 February 2008; *What is shared space?*, Hamilton-Baillie Associates; the Shared Space Project, http://www.shared-space.org

84 *No Fear: Growing up in a risk averse society*.

85 *Why Things Bite Back*, Edward Tenner.

86 'Child safety has its own dangers', Dr Helene Guldberg, *Spiked*, 19 June 2001.